WHITMAN COLLEGE LIBRARY

D0956007

The Music Theater of Walter Felsenstein

"Es war so alt, und klang doch so neu!"
(It was so old and yet it sounded so new!)

Wagner, *Die Meistersinger,*
Act II

Withdrawn by
Whitman College Librar

The Music Theater OF Walter Felsenstein

Collected articles,
speeches, and interviews
by Felsenstein and others,
translated, edited, and
annotated by

PETER PAUL FUCHS

Copyright © 1975 by W. W. Norton & Company, Inc.
First Edition

All Rights Reserved
Published simultaneously in Canada
by George J. McLeod Limited, Toronto

Library of Congress Cataloging in Publication Data
Main entry under title:
The Music theater of Walter Felsenstein.
1. Felsenstein, Walter. 2. Opera—Addresses, essays, lectures. 3. Opera—Dramaturgy. I. Felsenstein, Walter. II. Fuchs, Peter Paul.
ML429.F43M9 782.1'071 75-6648
ISBN 0-393-02186-6

Printed in the United States of America
1 2 3 4 5 6 7 8 9

PENROSE MEMORIAL LIBRARY
WHITMAN COLLEGE
WALLA WALLA, WASHINGTON 99362

ML
429
.F43
M9

PENROSE MEMORIAL LIBRARY
RECEIVED

OCT 22 1985
86-1844
ACQUISITIONS DEP'T

Acknowledgments

My warmest thanks are expressed to all persons who gave their assistance to me in compiling the material contained in this book, and in enabling me to make the necessary accompanying studies. Particularly I should like to name Professor Dr. Walter Felsenstein himself; furthermore Stephan Stompor, leading Dramaturg of the Komische Oper; Joachim Herz, director of the Opera in Leipzig; Wolfgang Kersten, Intendant of the Opera Theater in Halle; and Staatsintendant Kurt Meisel of the Residenztheater in Munich. I am indebted to the Komische Oper for the photographs they generously contributed.

For putting the book into its final shape, special mention should go to my editor, Dorothy Curzon who gave unstintingly of her time and energy and patiently put up with my stubbornness on many issues.

December 10, 1974

PETER PAUL FUCHS

Contents

Foreword

by Peter Paul Fuchs

In the mid-fifties, when the cold war was still in progress, it was considered somewhat adventurous for the holder of an American passport to visit East Berlin. Not too many Americans did it, and consular officials frequently advised against it.

Among the Americans who did cross the border into what was then known as the Russian sector, many had a rather strong incentive: they were either opera professionals or dedicated opera fans. And what they expected to find in East Berlin was not just opera but a minor miracle. Word had been received from various sources about a new "magician" of the opera stage; at the Komische Oper there was a leading stage director named Walter Felsenstein, who was responsible for opera productions such as had never been experienced anywhere. However, these reports mentioned not only the excellence of Felsenstein's productions but also the "strangeness" of his working methods. "You know, he had a hundred and three rehearsals for *Magic Flute*" was the kind of awe-stricken remark one was likely to hear.

It must be remembered that in the fifties outstanding opera productions on the Continent were not hard to come by. West Germany had rebuilt most of its bombed-out theaters and had reestablished excellent and progressively oriented opera companies in many cities, even in some very small ones. New works were being presented, new techniques and new equipment experimented with, and in Bayreuth there was a new era: under the guidance of Wieland and Wolfgang Wagner a style emerged in the realization of Richard Wagner's works which, after being bitterly opposed at first, soon was imitated almost everywhere.

Then we heard about Felsenstein. His manner of presentation apparently was something completely different. When I told friends who had been to his theater about my being greatly impressed with certain productions in West Germany, I would usually get the smiling answer: "Wait until you see your first Felsenstein production. You will forget everything else."

Unfortunately, another dozen years had to pass until I had an opportunity to witness Walter Felsenstein's work. In the meantime I read many reviews and heard many reports. All of them seemed to stress the fact that his work was based on realism. This was very puzzling to me, as it must have been to many others. Realism: was that not what all of us who considered ourselves progressives had been trying to get away from in opera? Had we not just learned from the Wagner brothers that one can present a dramatically overwhelming performance on an almost empty stage, with light taking the place of most of the conventional trappings? Realism in opera, as it was known in the United States in the forties and later, was nothing less than the defense of the indefensible. It was a stubborn attempt of conservative—not to say lazy—designers and directors to prove that all visual stylization was nonsense, that every house, tree, or mountain on stage had to be presented as a true likeness of nature (or at least as true as their inadequate techniques would permit). When a large tree was needed, a crew would be kept busy for at least a week, cutting out and painting all the little paper leaves. And the "magic fire" in *Walküre,* with its thousands of strips of red tissue paper and its dozens of electric fans, was truly a "magic" feat of engineering.

The irony was that with some of these "realistic" directors of the past their realism encompassed sets, costumes, and lighting, but left the performers and their "standard" operatic gestures almost untouched. I remember one stage director who would spend sleepless nights over the placement of every little glowworm in the first act of *Butterfly,* but who on the other hand would shrug off the most amateurish excesses of anti-acting on the part of his singers. Apparently, the sets in that type of production *had* to be done with love, not in order to furnish the proper framework for the action but to divert the spectator's attention from the atrocities committed by the singers under the collective name of "acting," or "scena," or whatever they called it.

Needless to say, this was not Felsenstein's kind of realism, as I found out when I attended my first performance at the Komische Oper in 1969, Offenbach's *Tales of Hoffmann.* The experience was quite overwhelming, and nothing that I had heard or read before seemed exaggerated. What I saw and heard that night could be called total theater. There was not any particular element that stood out; everything fell into place and contributed to a performance that felt right from beginning to end. Singing, acting, sets, costumes, lighting, orchestra, chorus, dancing—all seemed to work together and to serve one common purpose. Of course, one might have disagreed with a number of details of the conception, but one had to admit that this interpretation was consistent and always made sense, and also that it was technically and visually brilliant. If this had taken 103 rehearsals to prepare (a number for whose accuracy I cannot vouch), chances are that not one minute of it was wasted.

But this is what surprised me most: realism in the Felsenstein sense has little to do with the way the leaves on a tree are painted —at least initially and superficially. It is the psychologically truthful adherence to the plot, and this truth must become evident in every detail of the production. Naturally, sometimes the plots of operas or musical plays are fantasies. In that case the realism becomes fantastic realism, and this will show not only in the acting but also in sets, costumes, and lighting. Thus we find a great deal of visual stylization (but never to the point of abstraction) in Felsenstein's productions, which in turn means that his realism is spiritual, and that it is far removed from the brick-upon-brick realism—perhaps "aborted naturalism" might be a better term—that we had come to know in our traditional opera staging. For instance, in Felsenstein's staging of Britten's *Midsummer Night's Dream* the fantasy is driven to such a point that the trees, shrubs, and ferns in the forest come to life. This is also realism, because it corresponds completely with the psychological reality of the story.

All this sheds new light on such terms as "stylization" and "symbolism." Before I had been to the Komische Oper I believed that Felsenstein's "realism" was the exact opposite of Wieland Wagner's "symbolism." Later I learned that this was far from true, and that the difference between these two great artists was one of emphasis and of working method rather than of philosophical background. For it seems to me that the driving force, the guiding principle, in each case is one of carrying the message of the piece across to the audience. Felsenstein does this mainly by the behavior of the acting and singing human beings on stage (although, needless to say, he adjusts the framework into which they are set with extreme care), whereas Wieland Wagner works rather by means of pictorial visions into which the characters are fitted. However, in either case the old opposition between "stylized" and "realistic" seems to have lost its meaning, for it is perfectly possible to be stylized and realistic at the same time; the stylization of the visual presentation, at least in certain cases, does not counteract the psychological realism of the drama. In fact, one is directly related to the other.

After my initial experience I returned to the Komische Oper several times, for another half-dozen performances. They covered a wide range of repertory, but the genuine theatrical excitement that permeated them was always the same. My interest in this style of presentation grew steadily, and I also was offered the opportunity to study some unpublished typewritten rehearsal reports, which shed a great deal of light on the workings of Felsenstein's method. However, my greatest acquisition of knowledge came from a meeting with Felsenstein which occurred in 1971. The occasion was a seminar that he offered at Boston

University, where I was unexpectedly pressed into service as his interpreter; this kept me at his side for the better part of three days. During that time, which was devoted to the study of two rather brief sections from *Traviata* and *Otello,* I was most impressed with his almost unbelievable perseverance in his work with singers. Instead of telling them what to do, he would guide them by means of complicated psychological processes, in order to have them discover the correct solution for themselves.

Since the various articles, speeches, interviews, and reviews in this book were written or delivered in different places and at different times, and also for different purposes, it was obviously impossible to arrange them in the order of a textbook, progressing from the simpler to the more advanced, and thereby familiarizing the reader gradually with the techniques of the music theater. Each contribution must be considered a little world in itself. This makes a certain amount of repetition of the technical substance inevitable, in spite of my attempts to eliminate redundancies. On the other hand, technical terms may suddenly appear in the text without having been explained beforehand. For that reason I thought it best to offer a few clarifications of terminology, as an initial orientation. This may quite possibly result in some further repetition of material, for which I am asking the reader's understanding.

The term "Musiktheater," which for our purposes will simply be translated as "music theater," means of course more than just "theater with music." Felsenstein uses the term to designate a theatrical work (or performance) in which dramatic and musical elements are used so as to melt into one another, and to create the total impression of a "seamless unity." This means that music is not to be used merely for the sake of variety, or to create a mood, and that singing is not to be understood as "exalted speaking," but that there must be an inevitability in the use of both music and singing. According to Felsenstein, the actor sings when his emotional state has reached an intensity that can no longer be conveyed through speaking, making the singing expression not just an increase over the speaking expression but a totally different type of communication. This implies, of course, that works in which there is only singing and no speaking must move on a higher emotional plane than those in which singing and speaking alternate with each other.

But can any work that uses only singing be performed on a consistently high emotional plane? Of course not. And this is one of the reasons why "music theater" means more than just theater with music: in order to be suitable for a music theater performance, the repertory must be chosen very carefully among works that offer the qualities required. Works in which singing is merely a tradition and not a psychological necessity are of little or no interest to the music theater producer. In other words, the work itself must be of such a nature as to make the unbroken continuity possible. If the change from speaking to singing appears artificial, or if the singing lacks inevitability, then there is little hope that in performance a total theatrical experience will take place.

Even though this factor is very important, it is not the only criterion for acceptability that the music theater imposes. The first carrier of dramatic intensity is the story, or plot ("Fabel," as it is called by most Felsenstein disciples). This plot must be unconditionally believable, or "realistic." However, in the interpretation of the word "realistic" lies the greatest potential stumbling block for the English or American reader. A "realistic" plot in the sense of the music theater is not necessarily one that happens to people we might know, or that could happen right here and now; it is merely one that is *believable on its own terms.* The plot of Berg's *Wozzeck* is realistic, but so is the plot of Britten's *Midsummer Night's Dream* or of Mozart's *Magic Flute.* Undoubtedly one of the greatest surprises to many observers came when Joachim Herz recently presented both *Rheingold* and *Walküre* as realistic pieces in the sense of the music theater and found wide acceptance with them.

If the term "realistic" covers such a wide range, the next question is obviously what type of plot is not considered realistic, according to the rules of the music theater. The answer is that the type of musical play or opera that does not lend itself to the realization of a total theatrical experience would fall into this category—for instance, certain Italian operas of the early nineteenth century in which the display of vocal bravura is the paramount purpose—but also operettas and musicals that neglect the cohesive plot in favor of arbitrarily interspersed, applause-drawing songs and production numbers.

Summing up, we may say that the music theater requires a thoroughly believable realistic plot, with intellectual and emotional qualities that reach the audience in the shape of legitimate theatrical experiences.

How are these experiences conveyed to the audience? Primarily by means of the acting and singing human being. In the music theater the singing actor is the center of all activity. He must not simply be a trained instrument of the whole artistic organism; he must function on the basis of his own spiritual understanding of the work, and the ability to make it perceptible *(ablesbar)* to the audience. (Absolute clarity of the action is one of the tenets mentioned over and over again.) In this ability the actor should be *guided* by the conductor and stage director but never *dominated* by them.

One of the essential ideas on which the music theater is based is that of teamwork. Its fundamental law is the establishment of a correct relationship with the partner. The singing actor in the music theater must not sing *at* his partner (or at the conductor, which is worse) but convey a message to him, a message to which the other person naturally must react in psychologically meaningful ways. This message must never appear to the audience to be "studied" or "memorized." It must seemingly be created spontaneously, on the spur of the moment, giving the impression that the singing actor is not playing an assigned role but is creating this role as the action develops.

However, in all this seeming improvisation there must be nothing willful or arbitrary. "The first and most important stage director is the composer" is the way Felsenstein puts it. Everything that is done onstage by any of the participants must be based on a thorough and exact knowledge of the score. For if a work is eligible for the music theater, every detail of its musical score is meaningful and must in some way be interpreted by the singing actor. For instance, the expressiveness of the singing actor must be uninterrupted; it must not start when he opens his mouth to sing. The orchestral interludes are indictators of his psychological state, and therefore he must be aware of every note that is played while he is onstage.

Of course, the dramatic interpretation of musical interludes by the singer is nothing new. But there is one detail not generally mentioned, which I think Felsenstein has described most graphically: if the singer is psychologically and physically aware of the quality of the orchestral interlude before he starts to sing, then as a result he will breathe correctly—that is, in a fashion which automatically gives his sung phrase the proper meaning and expression.

Felsenstein is a sworn enemy of everything that smacks of routine or cliché. He feels that the director must interpret the libretto and the score in a logical and consistent fashion. Therefore, no extraneous effects or gags are permitted, no matter how traditional they may have become. In some standard operas this may result in the complete rebirth of certain characters that had been taken over by stale routine. But it is never done with the intention of just being different or original; the cardinal purpose is always to follow the author's intentions. This is a laborious and time-consuming process, but no one I know has ever denied that the results are rewarding. The effects of rethinking become even more apparent in the work with the chorus. In the music theater, the chorus is not a faceless mass; it consists of distinct individuals, each with his own personality and ideas. There is never any evidence of "Second tenors, move to the right at the start of the Allegro," as we find so often in routine performances. In fact,

Felsenstein goes one step further by avoiding the term "chorus" completely, and always referring to the choristers at the Komische Oper as "Chorsolisten" (chorus soloists).

One more element that is indispensable in the music theater is the "partnership with the audience." This means, according to Felsenstein, that it is not simply the spectator's function to watch the stage action silently, and be more or less satisfied when it ends. It means that from the very start he must be drawn into the action and become part of it. This, of course, can happen only when the actors onstage can make the spectator forget that they are performing roles, and plausibly become human beings who convey to him their thoughts, passions, and experiences.

There is no need to point out that in an art form as precise and exacting as the music theater, sets, costumes, and lighting must be attended to with the same loving care as the action itself. What should be mentioned, though, is that in this "realistic" form of the theater the visual elements are in no way limited to manifestations of a narrowly realistic nature. Again, the intention is not that of a pictorially faithful reproduction of life. The music theater never tries to deny that it is conscious theater, and not a lifelike illusion. It is therefore free to use all theatrical effects, including stylized sets, area lighting, and so on, to the best of its abilities, as long as the result remains true to the message of the piece presented.

In view of such uncompromising principles, it is certainly of interest to know the working methods by which these principles can be put into practice, and the high standards maintained. These methods are vividly described by Stephan Stompor, Dramaturg of the Komische Oper.* Here is how he sees it:

*Some readers in the Western hemisphere may not be familiar with the term *Dramaturg*. Every major German theater, whether legitimate or opera, has one or more Dramaturgs on its roster. Their tasks are, among others, to do research on the source material of plays, write the program booklets, make preliminary selections of new works to be performed, and take care of publicity.

Coming to grips with a work to be presented begins in our theater with joint readings that precede the placing of the work in the repertory. Further readings and working conversations take place several months before the beginning of the rehearsals, and are used for the analysis of the work and the discussion and clarification of the staging conception. Participants in these conversations are the stage director, the conductor, the set designer, the members of the dramaturgy, the assistant stage directors, the chief of musical studies,* the chorus director, and the assistant conductors. Once the musical rehearsals start, the conductor, coaches, and chorus director already possess a thorough knowledge of the work, jointly acquired, and a clear idea concerning the intentions of the staging. On this basis they commence their work with the singers.

The transition to the scenic rehearsals (generally three to six months before the opening date) happens quite smoothly, often in the form of reading rehearsals with the participants seated at a table, where the work is sung with piano accompaniment and discussed, and with talks about the individual roles. Then there is a complete introduction, during which models of the sets and costume drawings are shown. Starting with the very first scenic rehearsal, a precisely marked basic construction of the set is provided, and technical personnel are also included in the process from the very beginning. The conductor participates in all scenic rehearsals. If the conducting of a performance or an orchestra rehearsal prevents him from attending, he is represented by the chief of musical studies, who during the process of rehearsals becomes an important partner of the stage director. All assistant stage directors are given clearly outlined assignments that involve them creatively and critically in the staging process. Parallel with the scenic rehearsals further musical rehearsals are held.

The working operation is not finished with the premiere; even afterward scenic rehearsals are held that serve to deepen and correct the interpretation. If an opera remains in the repertory for a long time, there will be "regenerative" rehearsals from time to time, in order to preserve the precision, freshness, and spontaneity of the performances. Every performance is critically observed by

*"Chief of musical studies" is my own translation of the standard term *Studienleiter;* in every German opera theater he is the senior assistant conductor, who is responsible to the conductor for the entire musical preparation of the solo performers.

> the stage director and the chief of musical studies, both of whom file performance reports. As a basic rule, every performance must be of premiere quality and must be able to convey the content of the work in the sense of the prepared conception, and in an animated and intelligible fashion. On this basis there can be no changes in cast, except where a second artist has participated in the entire process of regular rehearsals.

According to this description it stands to reason that generous amounts of time are needed in the preparation of a music theater staging. And yet, Felsenstein himself resents it when someone faces him with stories about a "legendary" number of rehearsals in his theater. He told us in Boston that he has a fairly exact formula for gauging the time needed: every stage work requires an amount of time for scenic rehearsals (not including, of course, musical rehearsals or the final orchestra rehearsals) equivalent to 100 to 120 times the actual playing time of the piece. Thus an opera of two hours' duration would require between 200 and 240 hours of scenic rehearsals. This is certainly generous but not exactly "legendary."

The question is asked very often whether the techniques of the music theater are really so new, and whether Felsenstein in his twenty-five years at the head of the Komische Oper has created something that did not exist before. The answer is, of course, that he has not, and that he never claimed he had. Music theater—as Joachim Herz puts it—was not invented by Felsenstein. It was invented by Monteverdi and Gluck, by Mozart and Verdi, by Bizet and Mussorgsky, to name only a few. Felsenstein simply rediscovered certain values which had been neglected in the routine of day-to-day opera performance and he put them into a system of great logic and consistency. Many people, particularly actors of the legitimate stage, will tell you that most of these principles can already be found in the writings of Stanislavski. This is also true, and again, Felsenstein and his followers have made no secret of it. It seems to me, however, that in one very significant respect

Felsenstein has gone far beyond Stanislavski: whereas Stanislavski's system was developed for the actor on the legitimate stage, and only in his later years widened to some extent so as to include the opera singer, Felsenstein's system is based on "the singing human being" and as such it deals directly with the problems of the musical stage. The great psychological importance of this difference is that according to Stanislavski the singer might learn how to speak a line with the proper expression and then learn how to sing it, whereas in the world of Felsenstein's music theater the sung line could never be spoken since it is based on an entirely different psychological motivation. ("The singing actor must prove to me that he has no choice but to *sing* the line.")

It is a fact that even now, after more than twenty-five years of continuous performance practice, the techniques of the music theater are not universally accepted, and that the instances where they have produced their best results are still relatively few. However, the main reason for this is undoubtedly the uncompromising attitude which they require from the performer, and the comparatively great amount of rehearsal time needed to carry them out successfully. Yet it seems to me that most unbiased observers will freely admit the great value of these techniques in the training of singing actors, and in generally raising the standards of our performances on the musical stage. For that reason it is my hope that this small volume may be considered a contribution even by those who might look upon Felsenstein's productions as a Utopia never to be reached under ordinary conditions.

Baton Rouge, Louisiana
July 12, 1974 PETER PAUL FUCHS

Prologue

(Excerpts from an article written by Felsenstein for the periodical *Das Schönste,* 1957, and from his introduction for the yearbook of the Berlin Komische Oper, 1958)

Ten years ago, in the auditorium of the former Metropol Theater, which had been heavily damaged in the war and was still surrounded by scaffolds, I was handed the title to the Komische Oper, then being founded. The project I envisioned then is one we are still trying to carry out: neither a third opera theater nor an equally superfluous second operetta theater should be opened in Berlin, but a new and genuine music theater.* In giving equal weight to "music" and "theater," I was trying to remove the dividing line that exists between the terms "opera" and "theater."

The working principles that came out of this were not my invention. Rather, they represented the sum total of efforts that were decades, even centuries, old and that are discussed, for

*During the late twenties and early thirties, the city of Berlin had three opera theaters: the State Opera "Unter den Linden," the Municipal or Charlottenburg Opera, and the Kroll Opera. When the Reichstag burned down in 1933, the German parliament was assigned the building of the Kroll Opera, which had already ceased to function as a theater due to political pressures. The other two houses were closed by government decree in 1944. In 1945, after the end of World War II, both resumed operations fairly promptly, although in other buildings, since their own theaters had been destroyed by bombs. Therefore it would have been logical to refer to the Komische Oper as the "third opera theater." Ed.

example, in letters by Gluck, Verdi, and Tchaikovsky, who rebelled against the "concert in costume," the vanity of the singers, and the "routine" presentation of opera. [See note following the Prologue.] But we did augment those efforts by standing firm and being willing to make sacrifices—necessary ingredients for the accomplishment of our aims within the framework of a permanent musical theater organization. We have also worked for public understanding in order to develop higher theatrical standards in our audiences. The realization of our aspirations requires a careful examination of every stage work to see that the music and dramatic action are truly complementary; frequently it entails restoration of the original version of the work. It prohibits any mere "guest appearance" of a star singer as well as any change in cast without our usual rehearsal period.* Through such masterworks of music and drama as *Carmen, Der Freischütz, The Bartered Bride, The Marriage of Figaro,* and *The Magic Flute,* we have developed working methods which we are now able to apply to a much wider range of the repertoire.

I should not like it to appear that our efforts on behalf of the musical theater are limited to opera only. I should much rather have those efforts understood as part of the great movement which from the manifold specializations of the performing arts reaches back to the universality of the theater—to its versatility and power, which were always greatest in times when, utilizing the inherent accord between stage and audience, the theater was able to proclaim itself an indispensable institution and a manifestation of public life.

*I know a true story which is not astonishing when you are familiar with Felsenstein's working methods, but which is often greeted with disbelief by American opera lovers. One time, on the day of a *Traviata* performance at the Komische Oper, the singer who was to portray Annina became ill. Since there was no one in the ensemble who had rehearsed the role, Felsenstein canceled the performance. He knew that any last-minute substitute from another theater, no matter how well prepared, would have destroyed the dramatic unity and meaning of the production. Ed.

This movement has no name and is certainly not organized, but it has obviously existed for a long time—whether as a result of methodical planning or of accident—in all branches of the theatrical profession, and it is inevitably reflected in the public's attitude. Influenced by the evolution of film, radio, and television, the theater is taking stock of itself, an act of self-preservation as much as a yielding to the demands of its audience.

It is not true that the technologically created visual and acoustical media alienate the public from the theater. On the contrary, they increase its sensitivity, discernment, and expectations. How else can one explain that the receptivity to theatrical offerings—meaning all kinds of theater—is greater today than ever before? More people have developed more exacting standards and there is, consequently, a stronger likelihood of disappointment.

The public has learned to discriminate. A new audience, incorruptible and endowed with an astonishing instinct, seeks a real theatrical experience behind the facade of our theaters, and all the expressive techniques of the performer—mime, speech, singing, dance—are equally appreciated. If, however, the theatrical experience does not materialize as anticipated, the audience will have no understanding of the presentation and will refrain less and less from giving vent to its outright disapproval.

The diversity of poetic expression, of the means of performance, and of the scenic presentation techniques during the past hundred years has not only led to a complete separation between spoken and musical theater but it has also created special categories within both fields. These tend to move away from one another with increasing determination. This results in skewing the actor's horizon; while the theater is seemingly being enriched, the scope of the actor's expressiveness is being impoverished, and the "play and counterplay" suffers.*

To implement the fruitful development of diversity in the theater, it is essential to set boundaries between trends, directions,

*For a more detailed explanation of "play and counterplay" see *Partnership with the Audience* on page 26. Ed.

and methods. Yet it is equally important that these should reinforce rather than obscure each other. Poetic truth has no use for banality or soporifics. Its language and expression cry out for music, and its music cries out for a spiritual and dramatic conception. We must not build fences between these elements; rather, we must seek out and promote the theatrical experience in every form of its existence.

EDITOR'S NOTE: The following quotations from Gluck, Tchaikovsky, and Verdi are illuminating reminders of the attitudes of these composers.

1. Gluck*

(From the dedication of *Alceste*):

> When I undertook to write the music for *Alceste*, I resolved to divest it entirely of all those abuses, introduced into it either by the mistaken vanity of singers or by the too great complaisance of composers, which have so long disfigured Italian opera and made the most splendid and most beautiful of spectacles the most ridiculous and wearisome. I have striven to restrict music to its true office of serving poetry by means of expression and by following the situations of the story, without interrupting the action or stifling it with a useless superfluity of ornaments; and I believed that I should do this in the same way as telling colors affect a correct and well-ordered drawing, by a well-assorted contrast of light and shade, which serves to animate the figures without altering their contours. Thus I did not wish to arrest an actor in the greatest heat of dialogue** in order to wait for a tiresome *ritornello*, nor to hold him up in the middle of a word on a vowel favorable to his voice, nor to make display of the agility of his fine voice in some long-drawn passage, nor to wait while the orchestra gives him time to recover his breath for a cadenza.

*Reprinted from *Gluck*, by Alfred Einstein, translated by Eric Blom, by permission of J. M. Dent & Sons Ltd.

**Note that Gluck uses the words "actor" and "dialogue" rather than "singer" and "recitative." Ed.

2. Tchaikovsky*

(From a letter to Nadejda von Meck, after attending a performance of Marcetti's *Ruy Blas* at the Teatro Dal Verme in Milan, 1877):

The performance was worse than mediocre. Sometimes it awoke sad thoughts in my mind. A young queen comes upon the stage, with whom everyone is in love. The singer who took this part seemed very conscientious and did her utmost. How far she was, however, from resembling a beautiful, queenly woman who has the gift of charming every man she sets eyes upon! And the hero, Ruy Blas! He did not sing so badly, but instead of a handsome young hero, one saw—a lackey. Not the smallest illusion.

Then I thought of my own opera. Where shall I find a Tatiana such as Pushkin dreamed of, and such as I have striven to realize in music? Where is the artist who can approach the ideal Onegin, that cold-hearted dandy, impregnated to the marrow with the fashionable idea of "good tone"?

(Letter to N. von Meck, after attending a performance at La Pergola in Florence, 1878):

What an incredibly poor performance as regards orchestra and chorus! The staging, too, was wretched. Such scenery in the town where Raphael and Michelangelo lived!

(Letter to S. Taneiev, 1891):

The question "How should opera be written" is one I answer, have answered and always shall answer in the simplest way. Operas, like everything else, should be written as they come to us. I always try to express in the music as truthfully and sincerely as possible all there is in the text. But truth and sincerity are not the result of a process of reasoning, but the inevitable outcome of our inmost feelings. In order that those feelings should have

*From Modest Tchaikovsky, *The Life and Letters of Peter Ilytch Tchaikovsky,* ed. Rosa Newmarch (New York, J. Lane, 1906).

warmth and vitality, I always choose subjects in which I have to deal with real men and women, who share the same emotions as myself.*

3. Verdi**

(Letter to Giovanni Ricordi, in reference to the impending staging of *Stiffelio*, 1851):

> There should be neither alteration nor expurgation, and everyone must really put his best effort into it. It must particularly be noted that, in the final scene, the effect depends on the manner in which the chorus is distributed about the stage, so they must have not just one stage rehearsal as usual, but ten or twenty if necessary.

(Letter to Countess Maffei, after attending several performances at the Paris Opera, 1854):

> It was at the first performance of this *Etoile du Nord*† and I understood little or nothing, while the good public here understood everything, and found it all beautiful, sublime, divine! . . . And this same public, after 25 or 30 years, has not yet understood *Guillaume Tell*, and so it is performed in a bungled fashion, mutilated, with three acts instead of five, and in a production unworthy of it! And this is the world's leading opera house.

(Letter to Vincenzo Luccardi, 1851):

> I know that not only *Stiffelio* was ruined in Rome, but also *Rigoletto*. These impresarios just aren't intelligent enough to understand that, if operas cannot be performed exactly as their composers intended, then it is better not to perform them.

*No wonder Felsenstein states that he did not invent the realistic music theater! Ed.

**All but the last excerpt are from *Letters of Giuseppe Verdi*, selected, translated, and edited by Charles Osborne. Copyright © 1974 by Charles Osborne. Reprinted by permission of Holt, Rinehart and Winston, Publishers, and Victor Gollancz, Ltd.

†An opera by Meyerbeer. Ed.

(Letter to Vincenzo Luccardi, 1863)

The opera went well enough in Rome, but it could have gone a thousand times better if Jacovacci had for once got it into his head that, to have a success, you need both operas suited to the singers, and singers suited to the operas. It is true that in *La Forza del Destino* the singers don't have to know how to do *solfeggi,* but they must have soul, and understand the words and express their meaning. I am sure that, with a sensitive soprano, the duet in the first act, the aria in the second, the romance in the fourth act and, in particular the duet with the Father Superior in the second act, would all have been successful. There you have four numbers spoiled in performance. And four numbers are quite a lot, and can affect the fate of an opera!

(Letter to Giulio Ricordi, 1871):

You know the libretto of *Aïda,* and you know that the role of Amneris requires an artist of great dramatic feeling who can really hold the stage. How can one hope to find this quality in someone who is almost a newcomer? Voice alone, however beautiful (and that is difficult to judge in an empty room or theater), is not enough for this role. So-called vocal finesse means little to me. I like to have roles sung the way I want them, but I can't provide the voice, the temperament, the "je ne sais quoi" that one might call the spark. It is what is usually understood by the phrase "to be possessed by the devil."

(Letter to Opprandino Arrivabene, 1877):*

Malibran?** Very great, but not always great. Sublime at times, but sometimes in bad taste! The style of her singing was not very pure, the tone production not always correct, the voice shrill in the high notes. In spite of that a very great artist, marvelous.

*From *Verdi: The Man in His Letters,* edited and selected by Franz Werfel and Paul Stefan. English translation by Edward Downes. Published by Vienna House, Inc., New York. Reprinted by permission.

**The reference is to the famous soprano Maria Malibran (1808–36), daughter of Manuel Garcia, with whose company she appeared in the United States in 1825, performing Rosina in *The Barber of Seville.*

PART ONE

Felsenstein on the Music Theater in General

The basic tenets and problems of this theatrical art form, as explained by the author

1

The Staging of Opera

(Lecture given during a discussion on the occasion of a guest appearance of the Komische Oper in Paris, 1957)

Should a stage director be more concerned with the score or the libretto when staging an opera?

Should a singer concentrate mainly on his acting when doing a role or should his acting be dictated by vocal considerations?

Should an opera performance principally serve the interests of the music and singing or should these be completely integrated into the dramatic whole?

The theater has been raising these questions for years and the answers arrived at in many discussions have supported the doctrines of the music theater in a variety of ways.

When we look at the questions, however, the first thing that springs to mind is that we are already used to classifying theater and opera as two separate, basically different art forms. I believe that the questions emanate from increasing dissatisfaction with this separation. And since so many distinguished musicians and critics have called for a reform of opera—a reform that would close the gap between the two kinds of theater and imbue opera with a new dramatic spirit—I wonder why we have seen so few positive changes. There is a great deal of discussion on this issue and there have been many relatively successful practical experiments. But a convincing breakthrough into music theater has not yet occurred.

Why? I think I can list some of the reasons. Efforts in that direction originate only with people, in the audience as well as on the stage, who genuinely love the theater and therefore seek a pure theatrical experience in opera too. However, they often forget that the usual operagoer is not looking for this kind of experience and perhaps is not even aware of the possibility for it. The art of the theater has old and strict laws. One basic condition for the occurrence of a theatrical experience is that the spectator must be drawn into the dramatic happening, into the poetry of a stage action. Hence, intelligibility, plausibility, and absolute truth in a creative presentation are of the essence. The pure theatrical experience is not confined to any particular type of theater. It may take place in a pantomime, an opera, or an operetta as well as in a play.

If a genuine theatrical experience does not take place during the presentation of a play because either the action itself or an inadequate performance fails to establish rapport between the actors and the audience, then the audience loses interest. The performance of a good play can be spoiled by a poor interpretation, but similarly the performance of a weak play, through the actors' outstanding artistry, may become a memorable event.

The same naturally holds true for presentations in the musical theater. Here, however, even if a genuine theatrical experience does not materialize, the performance makes possible another kind of enjoyment. The joy in the sound of beautiful voices, in the animation of dance movements or of the musical show—these pleasures are completely legitimate, and the audience that expects them will in most cases be satisfied. They do not exclude a genuine theatrical experience, but they are not directly tied to it.

Like the works themselves, the performances of traditional opera are the results of a genuine demand, and sometimes they represent remarkable artistic accomplishments, even if not in a theatrical sense. As with every art form subject to changing times and changing tastes, these productions have their own development. Also, you will find in them great singing personalities who, outside the strict laws and in their own way, manage to communicate great theatrical experiences. The audience of the traditional form of opera is quite content and demands, in my opinion, no particular reforms and innovations. The singers are interested in improving their dramatic performances, to be sure, but their artistic and technical training usually is not a foundation for the working methods demanded by the strict laws of theatrical art.

Even the operatic repertory accommodates itself to these circumstances to a great extent, and certainly does not limit itself to operas which from a standpoint of form can be considered dramatically valid. Yet there are many works that are based on genuine vision, and whose development is in full accord with the laws of the theater. The music of these operas serves the dramatic action and situation exclusively; the singing serves no less exclusively as the actors' medium of expression. Interpreting such works as the creators intended naturally requires artistic personalities and working methods which are found only rarely in professional opera. Therefore the rendition in most cases falls short of the aims of the composer and the author.

If, however, these performances of great masterworks, although dramatically inadequate, are orchestrally and vocally exciting, then they may provide a pure joy for the lovers of beautiful music and beautiful voices which in their eyes will fully substitute for the theatrical experience, if indeed they have been looking for it. On such occasions even the theatrical enthusiast may reap some reward, since these works legitimately belong to the great and true theater. Thus he can sense in their music a deeply felt human and dramatic declaration, even if it is not made obvious by the interpreters.

From these factors the paradox emerges that some masterworks of operatic literature are highly successful and yet have remained largely unknown because the creators' intentions have been incompletely communicated. It is quite possible that an outstanding conductor who can extract from an operatic score a veritable orgy of sound does not even feel the necessity of conveying the opera's dramatic message convincingly. Also, it happens frequently that singers are highly acclaimed for their beautiful voices and their dramatic temperaments but have not done justice to the creators' intentions.

The separation of opera and theater rests primarily on the banal but logical basis of supply and demand. Advocates of the consistent music theater should therefore not try to assert themselves where they are neither wanted nor needed and where most of the prerequisites are lacking. Rather, they should work together to achieve results helpful to our cause, compromising as little as possible. Even an audience which is extraordinarily receptive to our efforts can form an opinion only when we offer a really valid production.

There is another reason why until now the results have not kept pace with the demands for a renovation of the musical theater. Due to the difficulties and obstacles I have been talking about, many stage directors have concentrated their efforts on questions of style, on scenic and visual problems. The real music theater experience can be no more than stimulated by the stage director, and can merely be supported by artifices of staging. It can be transmitted only by the music-making and acting human being.* The experience takes place only when the dramatic function of music and singing is correctly defined and properly applied. This function is clear: to transform an action through music and singing into a theatrical reality that is unconditionally plausible.

*This is an expression of Felsenstein's campaign against the stage director who wishes to overwhelm the audience with a dazzling show, but who resigns himself to standards of mediocrity on the part of the individual actor. Ed.

2

Method and Attitude

(From a lecture delivered at the Academy of Music and the Performing Arts in Vienna, 1963)

Eleven years ago a group of journalists asked me to explain what we were trying to accomplish at the Berlin Komische Oper, which at that time was only four years old. This was my answer: "The heart of music theater is to turn music-making and singing on the stage into a communication that is convincing, truthful, and utterly essential. All problems of the drama and of staging are secondary to this. Music theater exists when a musical action with singing human beings becomes a theatrical reality that is unreservedly believable. The dramatic happening must take place on a level where music is the only means of expression. The performer must not give the effect of being an instrument or a component part of music that already exists, or of a marionette being manipulated by the music, but that of being its creative fashioner."

I do not believe that anyone could oppose this as a basic concept, not then and not now, but whether or not it is possible in a literal sense is a moot point. That everyone taking part in a performance is concerned with something so "unspeakably" significant and moving that he can communicate in no fashion other than by singing—when and where do you encounter that? It happens so seldom that of the vast majority of people who could undoubtedly respond to it, only a tiny fraction has actually undergone the incomparable experience of the music theater in its entire potential and still believes in it despite disappointment. A far greater percentage, which approves of our goals but has never seen them achieved and has observed over and over that they are either ignored or misunderstood by the opera houses, considers the experience a Utopian dream of professionals and intellectuals. The people in this category either become indifferent to opera or they abandon the unsuccessful experiment, and rightly so, in favor of the other pleasures of traditional opera performances.

This is the situation from the public's viewpoint, which at the moment seems more important to me than that of the professional, and which I should like to make the starting point of today's conversation.

The music theater's quality of accomplishment is still not high enough to change the situation. I do not want to underrate the achievements of the Berlin Komische Oper and other theaters, nor am I ungrateful for the unmistakable successes which confirm that we are headed in the right direction. But it cannot be denied that these achievements are not consistent and that the high level is maintained only rarely throughout entire evenings at the theater. In the clash of opinion between the adherents and the doubters, we can offer too little evidence to be convincing to the greater part of the public.

Our chief concern therefore, now as before, is with the "humanization" of opera, with the unification of human being and song. Not everybody with a beautiful voice has the talent to sing on the stage. Some lack the ability; others think they do not need it. And many who could become proficient in this type of singing have no voice.

A strong personality can help tremendously to close the gap between human reality and the artificiality of singing. However, as long as there is a dearth of great performing personalities with beautiful voices, the solution is to put the techniques of stage singing within the reach of those who possess good voices and who have, in addition, some talent for performance and for emotional expression. This may offend the voice pedagogues who are not familiar with our methods, but it is in fact an essential task that is far from having been accomplished.

If therefore, as it would seem now, our ambitions are stronger than the potential to realize them convincingly, consistently, and reliably, if the discrepancy between theory and practice cannot be overcome, then the danger exists that the principle itself—the idea of unity between music and theater—may be open to question.

For many years this unity has been preached and glorified. But let us be honest: when has it fully succeeded? When did it happen that the duality of music and scenario, of singing and acting, was completely eliminated? Only during rare and enchanted hours, for whose recurrence there is no guarantee. And are we working consistently enough toward the removal of this duality? I say no. The deeper you go into the complexity of combining acting and singing, the more keenly you will be aware of the existing division. Defining this problem, in my opinion, is the much neglected starting point for the advance from theory to practice.

Again and again I encounter in my work a mistake which is not only unconscious but which is not even known to be a mistake: to consider music as an existing reality rather than as a most unusual manifestation. What exists and is real? Certainly only the action, and the human situation that derives from it. This generates the emotional state of the performer, which in turn produces his further action. This state, however, is physical as much as emotional. Therefore even singing belongs to it and is subordinate to it. Yet I cannot believe this as long as the music-making and singing on the stage appear to be studied and reproduced from memory.

The actor must be able to make me believe that every statement of his stems from a motivation that I can recognize, and that only through this motivation his emotion grows to a point where he discovers singing, and discovers it in exactly the manner prescribed by the composer. You will agree with me that the greatest impediment to credibility on the stage, and to a true theatrical experience, is memorizing. In the opera this is no less valid than in spoken plays. Therefore the ability to find within oneself the correct motivation for every statement is the cornerstone for any working method; it is also the only guarantee to avoid memorizing.*

Only this motivation makes it possible for the performer to exert the essential musical leadership without which the dramatic credibility cannot be accomplished and the audience cannot participate. And what does musical leadership mean? Not just knowing the music well enough to become independent from the conductor, but *motivating* the instrumental portion.

The vocal line is only part of the musical message contained in the score, and not even always its most important part. Also, emotion does not arise independently but as the result of the total physical and psychological situation (under no circumstances a thought process). Thus, emotionally credible music-making is a creative act involving the entire physique of the performer and dominating the instrumental as well as the vocal portion of the score—a statement of the performer born out of action and emotion, and unusual in every respect, which makes him and the audience forget that he is a "professional" singer.

Consequently, he is obliged to make the concern of the character he is portraying so unconditionally and consistently his own that to him and to the audience all basic musical functions—rhythm, meter, harmony, tempo, dynamics—do not appear to be prescribed by the score or the conductor but seem to be determined by his, the character's, intentions and sensations. It is obvious that this must happen in strictest adherence to the score, since any arbitrariness could lead to a total misunderstanding.

*Let no one believe that Felsenstein's actors do not memorize their roles. What the author is campaigning against is not memorizing as such, but the *appearance* of having memorized. Ed.

Then perhaps it is a thought process after all, conditioned by technical consciousness and control?

Yes, but not a thought process of the actor as an individual, only of the acting character. All technical elements of dramatic singing, such as breathing, intonation, and rhythmic flow, are not simply outside the shaping of the role (and interfering with the spontaneity of expression) but are an integral part of the emotionally conditioned physical action. No performer will be able to conquer the duality of singing and acting who does not understand that rule and apply it consistently. Unfortunately, most of the voice pedagogues and artistic heads of theaters do not demand this integration—frequently they call it unrealistic—despite the fact that every great singing actor, without ever giving much thought to the matter, does it instinctively.

Naturally, committing a role to memory and adjusting vocally to the role's requirements are initially purely technical operations for the singer. But the longer he does these without a precise dramatic conception, the more the vocal preparation of a role, through force of habit, will turn into a vocal exercise (to which perhaps some content has been added), with beautiful sound and technical perfection becoming ends in themselves. Later, at staging rehearsals (or shortly beforehand) when the singer is familiarized by the stage director with a concept in whose origination he did not participate, singing and acting have already become two irrevocably separated functions which hinder one another. Although with diligence and skill a tolerable compromise can be managed, it will never be a convincing unity. For if the singer accepts the interpretation of the stage director, perhaps even embraces it with enthusiasm, then his acting—depending on talent—may acquire the dramatic expression but will cause vocal difficulties, since the vocal portion was prepared technically under conditions which no longer apply. The singing will lack the vocal drama that matches the action. If the singer is not convinced by the director's conception but does not want to give up the role, he will superficially follow the director's instructions, as long as they do not interfere too much with what he has worked out vocally in the "musical" rehearsals. In that case you will find a vocal exercise with superimposed, insincere acting.*

These contradictions may even multiply if the stage director and the conductor have not agreed on the interpretation before the beginning of the rehearsals. Their inevitable differences of opinion will be loudly expressed, with or without being resolved, and always to the disadvantage of the singer, who tries to follow instructions which contradict each other. Thus he is limited to obedience, and thereby to artistic impotence, or else he ignores the instructions of his torturers (and mostly also those of the composer) and presents himself as an unscrupulous vocal acrobat.

The singer should therefore prepare the acting concept as early as possible, and in any case before the text and music have become firmly imprinted on his memory. This concept must, of course, be based wholly on the score, and is usable only when it becomes binding for all participants in the production. Therefore it must be not only determined but also accepted before the beginning of the studies. Whether the stage director, the conductor, or the performer bears the most creative responsibility is irrelevant; the important thing is for all members of the team to make the concept their own, even the musical and vocal coaches. If it has been arrived at on the basis of a profound study of the work, if it is in accordance with the score in all details, and if all performers stand up for it with conviction, then there will be no utterance or action on the stage that is not based on the music. Every instrumental and vocal sequence is dramatic action, and all instructions pertaining to dynamics, meter, and tempo are primarily not technical but expressive indications. In short, *every-*

*In order to show his contempt for this kind of attitude, Felsenstein uses the word *Spielastik,* which is taken from the German theater jargon and defies translation. It implies a hollow, routine type of acting, which the performer himself finds slightly ludicrous. Ed.

thing visual is as much music as everything audible is action. The words "musical" and "scenic," as used to set boundaries between the fields of responsibility, have become expendable.

The singer will then no longer be the victim of different "conceptions"; by studying the score he enters more deeply into the intentions of the composer and discovers the vocal drama of his role. He is no longer merely obedient; he arrives at his own ideas and has a fair chance of fulfilling his creative assignment.

Of course, if a singer is too conscious of his vocal technique, it will hamper greatly his attempts to sing expressively; this hindrance can be avoided if he learns early in his musical studies how to execute all technical processes involved in the expression of any emotion demanded by the role. But that is impossible for him, in my opinion, unless he has acquired during his vocal training a concept of singing that is valid for him as an individual and that protects him during his entire career against accepting singing as routine, one that will always renew his wonder in singing.

From what I have seen in the theater I would guess that many voice teachers fail to examine a pupil's capacity to absorb experiences; nor do they get acquainted with his individual emotional disposition and potential and teach him during his vocal training how to make use of them in divers situations. By the same token they neglect to show him how to examine for himself the oneness of singing and acting. If the situation were otherwise, the majority of singers, sometimes quite talented, would not need to have their attention drawn to the correct utilization of their own emotional potential. Furthermore, we would not have to cope with the widespread opinion that a beautiful, well-handled voice alone justifies the singer's presence on an opera stage; were it not for this belief, we would have another criterion for the admission to vocal training, a new standard that would add substantially to the persuasive power and the popularity of the music theater.

The fact that very few opera singers seem to come to terms

with the divergent types of singing called for by various dramatic situations indicates that in learning a part vocally most singers fail to analyze the opera and to seek motivation for their singing, that they place more importance on vocal production than on the human statement. This will inevitably result in the tendency to treat singing as a "presentation," and after that it is a short road to complacency. Clearly in this sequence the performer feels no need to relate to his partner—an elementary condition for the credibility of a stage action—and, depending on artistic standards and sense of responsibility, the relationship will be either faked or completely ignored.

A good case in point is the aria of Mařenka in the first act of *The Bartered Bride.* If I may briefly recall the story: Jenik, the son of the peasant Micha, who years ago was sent away by his parents because they favored his stepbrother over him, has now returned unrecognized, as a farmhand. He and Mařenka meet and fall in love. Since he knows that Mařenka and his stepbrother have been promised to each other by the parents of both, he will not reveal his origin to her, in spite of her repeated pleas; this is partly in order to thwart the arranged marriage, partly to put her love to the test. Mařenka seeks him out and tells him in despair that she has just learned her engagement is imminent. His cautious equanimity and his renewed refusal to reveal his secret awaken in her the suspicion that he may be untrue to her.

"If I should ever find that out, I could never forgive you" is the beginning of her aria in which she, first begging, then insisting and desperate, finally with a threat of bloody revenge, tries to force an explanation out of Jenik. It is an extremely dramatic conversation of a passionate girl whose love, distress, and jealousy make her singing not only convincing but the sole possible means of expression, with a partner who by the dramatic situation is forced to be silent, and who maintains his silence in spite of his growing agony. A gripping duet for one voice.

If this scene does not succeed, because Mařenka is busy not with Jenik but with herself and, misled by the faulty German translation, performs this aria with a display of sentimental lyricism,* then it will not only result in a distortion of the sense of this composition but the relationship between Jenik and Mařenka as well as the entire subsequent action will become unintelligible.

[In the following paragraph the author cites Max's aria from Weber's *Der Freischütz,* an opera far more popular in Germany than elsewhere. According to Felsenstein, the aria is often presented as a melodious folksong, unproblematic, and directly addressed to the audience. In actuality, it is the almost feverish dream-vision of a young huntsman who finds himself in the most desperate situation of his life: he has failed in several shooting contests; now he is in danger of losing his fiancée, Agathe, unless he miraculously recovers his skill. He recalls his happier, more successful past in a dreamlike monologue, in the middle of which he suddenly plunges back into the harsh and threatening reality. It is an intensely dramatic situation and must not bring forth an empty vocal display.]

Mařenka's aria is an example of the concrete, conscious dramatic statement which from the recitative increases emotionally into the heightened arioso expression. Max's aria is an example of a dramatic situation in which the performer, in a trancelike state, is gripped by a process which—without his help, as it were —sings in him. I call this "mute" singing. Many more examples of "articulated" and "mute" singing could be cited. Yet in all cases it becomes evident that a musical-dramatic happening turns into a believable reality only when the music is presented not as something that already exists but when it seems (along with the words) to grow out of the performer's real or imaginary relationship with his partner, when singing is not a normal but a most unusual dramatic statement, and when music and singing are

*In several English translations of this aria that I have come in contact with, very little of the above-described emotional turmoil becomes recognizable. I suspect strongly that some of them may be translations not from the original Czech but from Max Kalbeck's German version, which Felsenstein finds so reprehensible. Ed.

communicated in such a fashion that the spectator absorbs them as action.

Admittedly, there are some "singers" on the opera stage, such as the tenor in the reception scene in the first act of *Rosenkavalier;* or there is singing as a means to an end, such as the aria Rosina sings for her guardian Bartolo, in *The Barber of Seville,* in order to lull him to sleep and divert his attention from her tête-à-tête with Lindoro; or singing as a quotation, such as the Antonia-Hoffmann duet in *The Tales of Hoffmann.* Yet in these and many similar cases singing could not be recognized as such if in the rest of the performance all utterances were presented as "singing."

There are undoubtedly many experienced opera singers, many more than the ones I know, who would theoretically agree with the approaches set forth here. Yet most of them would consider the goals technically unrealizable, or attainable only through working procedures too lengthy to be practicable for a theater or for themselves (in view of their financial interests). These people overrate the difficulties of the working method, because they are more bogged down in their routines and acquired principles than they care to admit, and also because they do not know that the appropriate attitude facilitates many things technically. However, both method and attitude are more easily come by during vocal training and early professional development than through a retroactive process upon later realization.

Thus the unity of music and theater is equivalent to the unity of expression and technique in a singing actor's performance. Accomplishing it is a matter of neither genius nor coincidence; it is learnable for any singer who is musically and dramatically gifted and has a beautiful voice. This unity is achieved when the dramatic action alone determines all vocal statements, and even the instrumental passages. Only then can the singer recreate a dramatically valid musical score exactly according to the intentions of the composer; only then will he appear sufficiently free and relaxed to turn everything in him and around him into music; and only then will he make singing actually his most convincing expressive device.

In that case the human truth of the event being portrayed and sung will attain such power of conviction that the spectator will be drawn into the metamorphosis as a co-actor, and will experience a more intense feeling of reality and community than he has known before—one which perhaps it is not even possible to experience outside of the theater.

3

Partnership with the Audience

(Lecture delivered during the master classes in Bayreuth, 1959)

All problems pertaining to craft and method in our profession should be viewed from the perspective of a partnership to which we are bound and through which the real theater actually came into existence, partnership with the audience. It is astonishing how many artists—particularly singers but also conductors, stage directors, and designers—ignore this basic premise or even consciously make light of it.

How can they do that and why are they allowed to do it?

Because many of them are totally unaware of the fundamental experience of the theater; and because a majority of people, on either side of the footlights, thinks that a presentation constitutes theater if it takes place on a stage, is accepted by the audience without protest, and is greeted with well-mannered applause at the end. Furthermore, the idea of a "theater for public benefit" —in lieu of the old court theaters, institutions now maintained by the state or the city—has in many places degenerated into a display of political rivalry.* A desire for cultural representation

*The author is referring here to a practice rather widespread in Germany, that two closely neighboring urban communities might, out of local pride, maintain theaters in competition with each other, where one theater could easily satisfy both communities. To most Americans the practice is bound to sound a bit Utopian. Ed.

among the cities caused more theaters to come into existence than could be staffed with first-rate artists. This did offer one advantage: theatrical performances became accessible to wider strata of the population. But instead of being satisfied with a repertory that could be handled by the available artistic personnel, many municipalities and theater directors gave way to the perilous ambition of performing not only spoken plays but also operas and operettas. They presented the most exacting works of the literature in all categories, even when they lacked the means to do justice to those works, claiming that this was the duty of "a place of cultural representation" or "an institute for artistic education." These pretentious titles enabled them to endow their efforts with a significance that might divert attention from some of the sins committed onstage and also helped them to justify a rather questionable self-assurance. On the other side of the footlights this attitude made it possible to turn the public's need for theater, which could not be satisfied in such a fashion, into a moral obligation to attend the theater. If someone insisted on protesting against this humbug with more than a few mild objections, he risked running afoul of the local patriots, and in the end probably found it wiser to subdue his genuine passion for the theater.

Events of this kind, which occurred around the turn of the century, fortunately no longer have any influence on the development of the theater. But even today they are numerous enough to color professional thinking within the theater, and to weaken and sully the concept of theater in the eyes of the public.

If a poetic work—verbal or musical—has not been completely and fundamentally understood by the producers, the possibility of a convincing interpretation onstage does not fully exist, and the audience cannot be affected to the extent required for a theatrical experience. In place of real knowledge of the work you will find a gimmick, the staging experiment that must be original at any price; in place of a valid interpretation there will be artistic egocentrism, exhibitionism, or even an amateurish approach. A seasoned spectator, looking for the true theatrical experience, will at first postpone judgment on this type of performance. After a while he will either reject it or, because he uses his imagination and wants to participate, he will derive increasing pleasure from details that have nothing to do with the work itself. The inexperienced spectator, no less receptive, will either feel no tug at his imagination and be bored or he will be misled by superficialities that appeal to him and will think that what he is watching is actually the play listed on the program.

In either case, there is an invisible wall between stage and auditorium, in spite of the open curtain, and the true theatrical experience is not taking place.

I have gone into all this because it explains why so many artists have been able to neglect the partnership with the audience. The absence of this partnership not only prevents the genuine theatrical experience from coming into existence but it even encourages the misuse of the theater for an endless variety of exhibition. The consequence is a spreading of ignorance concerning the meaning and essence of theatrical art.

A highly talented tenor was very successful in the leading role of one of my earlier productions. During one of the later performances the applause after the first act was weaker than usual.

"What kind of a stupid audience is this tonight?" the tenor asked me. He was worried and angry.

"The audience tonight is unusually good," I said.

"But there is so little applause," he replied, "and yet I feel I am in excellent voice. Don't I sound good?"

"Your voice sounds very good," I said, "but from the very beginning you lacked concentration." And I explained to him that his inner state had not communicated, that his expression frequently was not in accordance with the prepared conception, and that the audience did not quite follow the structure of this important and difficult act.

"But I sounded good, don't you think?" he said again. I left it until the next rehearsal.

A few years ago I crossed paths with a young stage director who had been an assistant in my theater, and whom I considered quite gifted. He told me proudly that he was in the process of staging *Lohengrin.* "How are you going to do it?" I asked him, genuinely interested in learning his viewpoint. I expected to hear something about his conception—the behavior of the chorus at the arrival of the swan, for example, or his ideas on the leading role.

"I am playing the work on a raked stage. Interesting, don't you think?" he said.

I proceeded to ask him about his family.

These are two small examples that indicate to what extent the opinions on meaning and essence of the theater may vary. And they prove how important it is these days to explain before beginning any theatrical discussion just what the term "theater" means to you.

"Why so complicated?" an impatient person might ask. "When I see a play acted, that is theater, and the other spectators and I are the audience. When I like it, I applaud, and when I don't like it I feel that I have wasted my money. What is all this talk about 'partnership' and 'fundamental theatrical experience'?"

Agreed, I shall say, but what do you like and what don't you like? As a performer I must know that.

I must also know how I must act in order to please you. Every process on the stage is an action which originates in the situation of one or several persons; it shows the relationships of these persons to one another—the conflicts and the resolutions or consequences of the conflicts. The more the action and the characters capture the imagination of the spectators and stimulate thought concerning their own lives, the more interesting the play will be found. Of course, the performance must be satisfactory and credible.

The good actor reveals to me the entire life of the character, beyond the stage action and the text. In this way he increases my involvement to a point where my own imagination makes the character even more real than his acting alone could do it.

We act together: thereby my existence as the spectator ends, and his as the actor; my consciousness that it is a play has disappeared, and I perceive the happening as more truthful than any reality. This metamorphosis, this fusion of play and counterplay, overwhelms the entire room. It is the real phenomenon of the theater, its own inalienable possession, unmistakable and eternal. This is what I mean when I say "partnership" and "fundamental theatrical experience."

In this connection it goes without saying that the music theater, without exception, is subject to the laws of the theater, only it is richer by one element than any other performing art and therefore carries a responsibility to a higher degree of effectiveness.

The additional element, music, determines more than any other the poetic message of this type of theater. Whether instrumental or vocal, it is the primary medium of expression in performance and it has no other function of any kind.

4

Basic Questions of Method in the Music Theater

(Lecture delivered at the International Theater Institute conference on contemporary opera interpretation, in Leipzig, 1965)

Since I presented my ideas fourteen years ago, a number of theaters have adopted the principles of the music theater; in their work they have arrived at conclusions which can now be grouped into a method. The periodicals, pamphlets, and books in which their conclusions have been reported could fill a small library. However, in reading this literature you may very well be misled into a belief that the basic requirement of music theater staging —to make singing and music-making into a convincing, truthful, and absolutely essential human statement—has already been fulfilled in many places.

It has not been fulfilled, either at the Komische Oper or anywhere else, but beginnings and partial success have demonstrated that it can be done. And wherever it has been even partially successful the reaction of the audience has always been positive. This reaction has provoked hostility in the practitioners of traditional opera, who sense in it a potential threat to the enthusiasm of their audiences, and many musicologists, who have tried to lay claim to the scores of *Don Giovanni* and *Otello* (among other operas) as absolute music, also disparage the idea. The attacks of these people are premature, since they are based on imperfections and misunderstandings of an approach to interpretation which is still in its beginnings. Among a hundred attempts there are perhaps five in which the singing on stage is genuinely a human statement and in which the integration of action and musical score is unmistakably recognizable.

In this quarrel with something that has barely come into existence, that is hardly even acknowledged, the defense is often forced to advance arguments which are based more on conviction than actual experience and therefore cannot always be proved. The disputes, oral and written, occur among critics, Dramaturgs, and writers, but seldom among conductors and stage directors, since they are usually too busy with practical work; and singers, who as a general rule are not interested in theory, hardly ever take part. The possible consequences are obvious.

The theorists—in their eagerness to create the necessary scientific basis for the practical accomplishments of the musical stage, to defend knowledge and principles against ignorance and hostility—will often indulge in such complicated debates that those for whose practical use they are intended can no longer follow. The theorists do not know enough about the perceptive capacity of the singer and his aesthetic background, and are in no position to influence or advance him in his methodic development.

On the other hand, the singing actor, because of his training and his professional background, is rarely independent in his artistic opinions or unrestrained in the utilization of his vocal and physical resources. For that reason he often feels overtaxed by the demands of a progressive opera stage, and at the mercy of the conductors and stage directors. If his self-confidence and his sense of responsibility cannot be bolstered enough for him to make his own discoveries and devise his own methods, then he cannot be depended upon as a creative interpreter. Whatever different opinions may be entertained concerning the contemporary interpretation of opera, no doubt exists that the focal center is the singing human being.

There is no gainsaying that a war is raging between the traditional and the new approach to opera, especially in matters of the musical action, the singing portrayal, and the function of music in the drama. It cannot be denied that isolated skirmishes and repercussions of this war can even be found in our own ranks. As long as the realistic music theater is incompletely realized in practice and lacks the power of conviction, theory gains in significance. If, however, the theory is formulated by those without stage experience, then the war takes place without combatants.

Before discussing basic questions of method I shall therefore first raise the issue of a new pedagogic quality in the training of the singing actor—the issue of the education of a rising generation which, aside from all interpretive abilities, must acquire a clear idea of its creative task, but which holds its own opinion in aesthetic questions and is in a position to establish the proper relationship between theory and practice.

I believe I can contribute best to this discussion if I limit myself to the presentation of certain problems which time and again remain unsolved. The first place is still occupied by the performer's separation of acting and singing—his difficulty, sometimes insuperable, in uniting expression with vocal technique. I am not speaking of untalented performers or of the victims of poor training but of persons whose acting talent, vocal quality, and intelligence appear sufficient to allow them to become useful performers in a music theater. With the help of good instruction, they have already established themselves in one role or another. But in every new production the same problem arises. If these persons find an intelligent, patient stage director who is experienced in dealing with singers, and a pedagogically inclined conductor, and if enough time has been allotted, then long, hard labors may bring forth a reasonably consistent result. However, that holds good only for the one production, and it depends strictly on the conceptions and methods of the conductor and the stage director.

If the same singers fall into the hands of a stage director who stresses his own dramatic and visual ideas to the point of overlooking individual shortcomings, or of a conductor who is only interested in realizing his own conception of the sound, the result, if not total disaster, may be at best a demonstration of impersonal drill. In either case a singer will find himself in an uncreative state of dependency. His memory is too heavily taxed to arrive at a credible personal statement, and therefore he is constrained to recite his role. Thus completely occupied with himself, he either neglects or simply fakes the relationship with his partner. The three deadly sins against creativity on the stage have been committed: lack of artistic freedom, recitation, and failure to relate to a partner. They have been committed not by an amateur—this would not be worth mentioning—but by someone who has learned from experience what these mistakes mean, yet lacks the strength to avoid them. Thereby he hinders his partner, who perhaps has already found the way to self-reliance through properly expressive use of his vocal technique; he comes in conflict with the stage director and, trying to follow the stage director's instructions, in conflict with the conductor. Depending on the size of his role, he impairs or endangers the entire production. As you know, this description fits the majority of the singers, even in leading theaters. From time immemorial, it has been only a small number of extraordinarily gifted people in whom the instinct for the poetic function of singing onstage could be awakened and developed from the very first moment of their training, and whose strong desire to express themselves enables them to subjugate vocal technique to expression without any difficulty.

It is manifest, however, that any musically gifted singer who possesses the ability to concentrate, who is above average in imagination, dramatic talent, and intelligence, and whose voice is healthy and not spoiled by faulty technical training, can acquire this ability. It is a question of his own energy and of the competence and patience of his teachers. He must learn, intellectually as well as through the proper exercises, to transcend the purely physical use of his voice: he must forget the *habit* of singing. Naturally, this does not mean to give up his regular vocal exercises, but these must be sharply differentiated from the poetically elevated, extraordinary statement—that is, the "absolutely essential" utterance of what cannot be expressed without music. The expressive exercises should contain every possible variety of feeling, in order to make it possible for every normal technique of voice production to adjust to any emotion. In contrast to his purely technical vocalizing, the singer should now feel a distaste for producing any tone that does not signify or express something definite. These exercises, if they are successful, will help him in two ways: the sound of his voice will become more beautiful and varied; and he will arrive at new accomplishments in range and dynamics that were not accessible to him through physical technique alone.*

Once he has acquired this basic attitude, he will be disinclined to memorize mechanically either music or text and will be unsatisfied to understand an action on a superficial level. While he examines the purpose of his singing, while he investigates why a certain phrase is composed in this manner and not in another, he discovers the motivation that leads to singing and discerns the intentions of the composer. He can no longer limit his interest to the vocal part: he feels the connection with the instrumental portion, the knowledge of the orchestral score becomes a vital necessity, and the danger of reciting has been eradicated.

The process of self-discovery, and the resultant feelings of enrichment and of a new creative power, cannot be brought about by the most elaborate explanations and instructions of the voice pedagogue, the stage director, and the conductor. Those instructions can and should complement, correct, and widen his own perceptions, but they cannot replace them.

The motivation for singing can, of course, take many forms—for example, the need to impart specific news, the need for reflec-

*The study of this last paragraph is heartily recommended to all those who insist that Felsenstein's efforts are exclusively directed toward intense and expressive diction, and that he is not interested in the sound of the singing voice. Ed.

tion; the occasion for singing might also be the unconscious projection of a strong emotional process or a monologue addressed to a vision. In any case it originates from a powerful urge to communicate, the nature of which determines the vocal usage.

But since every utterance must be related to something, the seeker cannot stop seeking. He finds the connection of his role with the actions of the drama, the relation to the other roles: he has begun to establish the creative independence so essential to the living music theater. In this process he may clash with the other performers, the stage director, and the conductor; he may merely cause friction or he may profit from the other points of view. Contrary to the conflicts of the singer who lacks personal freedom in his approach, however, these are creative conflicts that force him to become familiar with the entire work.

When you analyze a work carefully, you will find that the events and instructions in the scenario do not convey sufficient information for the complete shaping of a role, that actions and persons can be fully understood only through the ferreting out of the preliminary plot.* A major portion of the preliminary plot can be reconstructed from statements in the score that refer to the past; hypothesis must do the rest. To what extent the interpreters are willing to give free rein to their imagination in this respect is a question for their artistic conscience.

From the preliminary plot are drawn the relationships of the characters to each other as they exist in the beginning of the play,

*The preliminary plot *(Vorgeschichte)* is similar to, but not identical with, the exposition of the play. Whereas the exposition in the ordinary sense includes only information actually given by the actors onstage, the preliminary plot must often go much further; in fact, it must take over where the exposition fails. Perhaps this is one of the most striking elements in Felsenstein's technique: where other directors might be content to state that the plot is poor because it lacks psychological background, and nothing can be done with it, Felsenstein creates the missing data from his own imagination, yet with a meticulous avoidance of anything that might seem arbitrary or illogical. Ed.

the initial situation.* The characters confront each other with different, frequently opposite, interests and intentions. As they pursue their interests and carry out their intentions, their relationships with each other change; new dramatic situations result. The singer realizes that the processes which cause all this to happen are far more varied and complicated than is obvious from the music and the text. He realizes that whether he sings or not, he acts during his entire time on the stage. Only now does he learn what "action" really means.

The acting singer, the musical performer who has reached this degree of independence, can no longer neglect the relationship with his partner, which is one of the most important factors in the credibility of a performance. He will no longer "sing *at* his partner," but will, by singing, actually communicate with him. Nor will he sing to feed his own vanity; it will be beneath his dignity. He knows that vocal beauty ultimately derives from nothing other than the truthfulness of his human statement.

Of course, there are not very many musical performers on this high level. That does not mean, however, that the training of topflight artists for the music theater should be considered a Utopian dream. The demand for highly qualified singers has become far greater than the supply offered by the schools, whose curricula and teaching staff frequently are inadequate or else do not take into account the requirements of a contemporary interpretation of opera.

In the repertory theaters there are quite a few talented performers, but most of them, not having been sufficiently trained, do not find the proper guidance throughout their careers and are

*The "initial situation" *(Ausgangssituation)* is another concept that assumes enormous importance in Felsenstein's productions. Since he absolutely insists that every detail of the relationships as they exist in the beginning of the play be clearly understood by all participants, he avoids any impression of tentativeness when the curtain first opens, and imbues the opening of the work with a richness and intensity that makes the spectator feel as if he had already witnessed several acts of the same plot. Ed.

stifled by the number of roles with which they must cope. The complete mastery of an operatic role—beginning with the singer's discovery of his own vocal function in the role, through learning the control he needs for the stage and realizing the full extent of his task, to the process of rehearsing, and at last the readiness to perform—requires an amount of time which no theater has available, not even the Komische Oper. If our educational institutions and private teachers cannot begin to integrate the acting and singing abilities of their talented students, if the opera theaters will not create special seminars of a studio type with properly qualified instructors, then the present level of interpretation will probably not be raised within the foreseeable future. The reason is that a major portion of the time available for the preparation of a production must be used for elementary instruction, and only a small part can be given to creative rehearsals.

The fact that there are so few singers who are independent in the recognition of their tasks and in their working methods burdens the conductors and stage directors with a pedagogic responsibility which they may not wish or to which they may not feel equal. It also gives rise, depending on capability, ambition, and authority, to a usurpation of the limelight by either the stage director or the conductor—a situation which may provide operagoers with the sensationalism they are seeking but is not conducive to a valid interpretation of the work. All this is the source of well-known and completely unproductive conflicts between the conductor and the stage director, and also between the singer and either one of them—or perhaps both.

It goes without saying that the responsible artistic direction of an ensemble must be in the hands of either a theater-conscious conductor or of an extremely musical stage director; both of them, and only in conjunction with each other, are the guiding power. Yet the focal point of the operation must be the singing actor. Only the stage director who recognizes this commandment and obeys it will escape the temptation to stage himself rather than the work; and the conductor who must force himself to obey it, rather than feel it within himself, may be able to unleash virtuoso sound effects, but he will never really belong to the music theater.

In my opinion, there is no stage director of exactly the type the conductor would wish for, and no conductor whom the stage director finds entirely unobjectionable. But if these men are qualified to practice their profession, are loyal to the theater and at the same time feel a kinship with their ensembles, and are not away from their home theaters fulfilling guest engagements most of the time, only one basic element is needed for the possibility of a creative collaboration: the profound knowledge of the work that is necessary for a faithful interpretation. This means that neither of the men may assume he knows the work well enough to be able to dispense with a joint analysis just because he has conducted it or staged it before. Since it is impossible to know every detail of the composer's intentions in a masterwork, the chance of new discoveries—depending on the maturity and experience of the interpreter—is always a rewarding prospect. If either the conductor or the stage director is teamed up with a partner who has never done a particular work before, this will give him the opportunity not only to let his associate profit from his own experience but also to use the other's fresh, uncluttered viewpoint in order to recognize and correct some errors in his own interpretation.

In the joint struggle of the conductor and the stage director to make the work their own, there may be some violent and yet fruitful altercations. Enmity will not result from this unless vanity and the craving for recognition are stronger than creative concern. More than with magic tricks of stagecraft or the sorcery of virtuoso sound, both artists will prove their interpretive ability by their guidance of the singers and the creation of an ensemble consisting of independent individuals.

This cardinal task is neglected by many conductors and stage directors, partly because in their quest for personal success other working methods seem more profitable to them and partly because they are professionally and pedagogically inadequate. But if the conductor has a commitment to the formation of an artistically self-reliant ensemble, he must not only participate in the preparation of the work from the very beginning; he must also conduct all the performances and not allow any guest conductor or substitute on the podium. For during the performance the conductor is the only active stage director, the day-to-day defender of the validity and intelligibility of the conception, the mentor and friend of the independently creative singing actor.*

To produce and develop a valid conception collectively requires capabilities which even nowadays, when it is customary to overrate the work of the stage director, are being underrated to an astonishing degree on both sides of the footlights. Not only the administrator of the theater and the box office manager should work in the interests of the public but the stage director himself, beginning with the first conversation with the Dramaturg, during the first reading of the score with the conductor and set designer, and in determining the cast. It is not sufficient for the director to have an interesting view of the work and intriguing ideas of production; he must be able to challenge his musical and scenic collaborators as well as the performers to such a degree that their dedication to teamwork goes far beyond mere obedience or tractability.

The conception of a work can be made intelligible and convincing at the opening performance if the stage director's intentions are carried out. It can remain intelligible and convincing only if during the course of rehearsals it has become the individual conception of every participant, and if every participant defends it independently in every performance. This can be accomplished by a director who, no matter what his age and experience may be, strives for and obtains the trust of all his collaborators. Putting

*This adamant attitude toward substitute conductors stems from Felsenstein's conviction that one tempo too fast or too slow, one fermata too long or too short, may completely alter the flow of the scene and thereby ruin the performance. Ed.

aside personal likes and dislikes, he must allow the production to develop at its own pace and must not strive for effects which may be impossible or unnecessary and which have not been arrived at through the normal working process. He must possess practical stage experience, and he must be reasonably familiar with the techniques of singing and dancing as well as acting—not in order to show the performers how to play their roles but to be able to communicate in areas where words fail.

He must prevent the work of the set designer from becoming separated from the rest of the process. The set designer must share equal rights and responsibilities in the interpretive shaping of the conception, so that he will not be tempted simply to create "decor." Instead, he will take pains to create a spatial composition which not only makes the unfolding of the action possible but actually demands it, and will contrive visual accents that force the spectator into participation and into the correct assessment of the events onstage.

5

On the Training of Stage Directors for the Music Theater

(Report delivered to the Committee on the Music Theater, at the International Theater Institute in London, 1971; published in volume XI of the *Jahrbuch der Komischen Oper*)

In many of the countries represented here today the education of the rising generation of stage directors is surely considered as important as the development of singing actors and several different methods are being tried. The kind of training each of us favors for the stage director obviously depends on what we believe his job to be—a definition which has given rise to some conflict. One side believes that there is an obligation to carry out meticulously the intentions of the composer and the librettist, and the other opts for freedom of interpretation. Varying points of view are held not only in different localities; they are sometimes represented within the very same production group. I should not like to start any new controversies on this point, and therefore I shall refrain from comment. In any case, the method of training relates directly to the method of interpretation.

I can only begin with the basic rule of my own work: the score and all the instructions contained therein must be unmistakably communicated to the audience; I am opposed to all arbitrary revisions, updated versions, and experiments that go against the character of the work.

However, independent of the difference of opinion concerning the stage director's goals and his field of activity, the method of training rests on how the work is to be communicated to the public and how much importance the director attaches to the singer in the dramatic concept and the staging. I am placing this problem in the foreground, since it is my feeling that the effectiveness of a music theater performance today is endangered, emotionally as well as intellectually, by the overemphasis on staging. I do not doubt that this is a minority opinion, but I can speak only within the framework of my own commitment and the experiences that have resulted from it.

For interpretations in which music and singing are used primarily as artistic conventions, and not as real, essential human statements, it is reasonable to regard the artist as an instrument, in the action as well as musically. In these cases a stage director with purely theoretical background would be adequate, as long as he is capable of transmitting his ideas to the performers. Performances as well as training within these boundaries are internationally accepted, and they are even valid, if they take place on a level commensurate with the work itself.

Things take on a very different aspect when an opera is produced according to laws of the realistic theater, when the boundaries between musical and spoken theater are abandoned to achieve universality of the theater. It is a task to which I have dedicated myself almost exclusively for a great many years, and I have tried during this time to make the theory of it clear, as well as illustrate it practically through my work. Whether or not it can be accomplished is open to controversy, and rightly so, but given the proper conditions I can prove that it is possible. (I realize that this is a biased statement and I ask your understanding.) This type of presentation, in my opinion, cannot be called successful until the division between stage and auditorium has been removed—that is, until the performance is powerful enough to move the audience, beyond any intellectual or critical judgment, to direct participation in the action.

As you know, this can be accomplished not through formal

devices of staging alone but through the effectiveness of the performer, who must appear to be creating the music as he sings. Naturally, that requires singers who are well chosen and specifically trained, but it also depends on a stage director who, profoundly familiar with the work, knows how to handle the singers for the best results. A singer who has been adequately trained can come to terms with a good stage director, even if the latter is not well acquainted with the traditions of singing and acting in opera.

But we are not here to discuss the quality of training available to singers for contemporary music theater production. Although there are many conflicting opinions, we can all agree on one point: only very rarely has a singer had the kind of training required.

For this reason the stage director's versatility becomes all the more important. Superb musicianship, theoretical knowledge of both music and theater, more than average imagination, taste, and psychological sensitivity: these prerequisites cannot all be acquired, but that they are fundamentals is not open to discussion. Three more things, although sometimes difficult to come by, can and must be acquired: knowledge of the work, communication with the performers, and the relationship with the audience.

As far as the knowledge of the work is concerned, we must remember that in a score created on the basis of a theatrical vision the music and technical instructions are only auxiliary devices for communicating the real intentions and the real content. This is the same as in poetry, where the words may be indicative of the poet's meaning but do not contain it completely. Without exact knowledge of the composer's and author's intentions the preparation of a valid, intelligible conception is not possible. I cannot speak for my colleagues, but I know that it sometimes is not until the second or third production of a work that I feel I have done the composer some justice. Whether the vacuum left by an incomplete recognition of the composer's intentions may be filled by the personal interpretation of the stage director is a question of the personal talent, the artistic maturity, and the sense of responsibility of the director. As far as I know there have been no substantial efforts until now to compile experiences related to these matters for the purpose of training. It is we, the stage directors, who are at fault, since we mostly limit ourselves to egocentric monologues, and do not take the trouble to share what we have learned.

The second chief problem is communication with the performer. We all know that a director whose conception is by no means outstanding but who understands how to work jointly with the actors toward its execution, and also knows how to express himself clearly, will produce far happier results than the one who is gifted with much better ideas but is unable to progress beyond theory in his contact with the performers.

For the incipient director knowledge of music and art history is indispensable, as is scientific knowledge, and these things are taught fairly well in the schools. But equally indispensable is personal experience in every aspect of staging, artistic as well as technological. Perhaps, due to a lack of sufficient information, I am now storming doors that are already open, but the performances on musical stages known to me mostly lead me to conclude that the director has not succeeded in giving the singer a feeling of creative significance, and that matters of lighting and other visual elements did not originate in close coordination with the acting, but evidently had been left to the discretion of the designer.

It is not sufficient to make the directing student work with beginning singing actors. He must, in order to put himself completely in the position of the performer, be able to cope with singing and acting problems, no matter what his ability as an actor or vocalist. For the point is by no means to show the singer how to act—this would in any case only lead to false imitation—but to know what can be expected from him, when it can be expected from him, and how one can facilitate for him the realization and intelligible execution of the action. If the director has not practiced these things himself, he may be misled into merely issuing instructions, ordering the performers around and gradually turning into an animal trainer on a pedestal.

Generally, applicants for stage directors' positions are assigned to theaters as assistants or residents, during or after their theoretical work, to gain practical knowledge. There are cases where this leads to the development of professional self-reliance. However, these cases are rare, and the creative independence is often dubious. An assistant's job can be most fruitful under an outstanding stage director, but only after a period of doing independent staging. By comparing renowned methods with his own experiences, the beginning stage director may gain the security on which to build the personal authority necessary to his position.

In places where it has been recognized that theoretical education should be simultaneously supplemented with practical study, it might be advisable to make use, in modification, of a method I once encountered in an acting seminar: the student directors share with a student conductor in the analysis of a masterwork of their own choice; after that, under the direction of one of the students, they study and perform (without an audience) a scene from that work, ignoring any lack of vocal ability. These exercises are continued until each student in the class has staged a scene performed by his fellow students. This proposition may sound absurd at first, but it is practical, in my opinion. In addition, a student stage designer could prepare models of stage sets, and the problems of lighting could be worked out with him.

If you agree that it is a good idea for the stage director to practice actual performance, not only to acquire authority but also to establish a good working relationship with his colleagues, you will also undoubtedly feel that he should have a certain amount of training in dance and body movement. For another thing, he must possess enough vocal knowledge to merit confidence in him when he advises the singers on vocal problems. This would put him more in touch with the voice teachers, whose customary unawareness in matters of staging endangers their students' security and independence. Through this contact the voice teacher would be induced to participate in scenic rehearsals at least now and then, and become better qualified to give support to acting as a part of singing.

I mentioned as the third chief problem the relationship with the audience. In connection with this we must ask to what extent the stage director realizes for whom he is producing. Directors differ widely on this. Here, too, I can only offer my own opinion: I think the music theater experience should be imparted to as wide and varied a public as possible. For that reason I demand from the stage director the ability to put himself at any time into the place of the spectator who is unfamiliar with the work and the performance, so that he will safeguard by every means available to the musical stage the intelligibility of the work and of the conception. At the same time he must draw from his audience not a passive reaction but an active participation. In practical terms this obliges the director to lead the rehearsals not only remembering what has gone before in rehearsal but also achieving a feeling of being absolutely uninformed.*

*Meaning a facsimile of the mental state of the spectator who is totally unfamiliar with the work. Ed.

6

The Approach to the Work: An Assemblage of Music Theater Problems

by Walter Felsenstein as told to Siegfried Melchinger

(From *Musiktheater,* published by Schünemann-Verlag, Bremen, 1961)

Every work that we perform must be transposed backward into a piece completely unknown to us; this is the lesson of innumerable past experiences. The misleading influences of established prejudices, faulty recollections, and erroneous teachings are unbelievable. What happened to me with *The Magic Flute* is example enough. Ever since the foundation of the Komische Oper I had been urged time and again to stage the work, and time and again I evaded it. I did not have the courage to confess to the friends and collaborators who pressed me that I considered it a bad work, which was the reason why I had never staged it before, and that in spots it even bored me. I had been infected by the general opinion that had arisen around *The Magic Flute.* You could read it everywhere: a stupid play by a theater manager from the Vienna suburbs, for which Mozart had written marvelous music; an impossible plot with a break in the middle. Something must have motivated Schikaneder while in the process of writing to transform the Queen of the Night from a good woman, as she was at first, into an evil one, and to turn Sarastro, who during the first act is a villain, into a kind man. I had accepted this belief without question, and no wonder; all the performances I had seen had been played in that manner. Just the same, in the long run I was unable to justify my reluctance, which I had never examined, and I had to make a thorough study of the libretto and the score of the work. We scheduled the opera, and at first we made no progress. But during our preparatory readings—I still remember the day—I jumped up in surprise and excitement. We had suddenly discovered a new piece that had never been played before, one evidently known until now to only one man, the one who wrote the music.

At that time I decided to believe no longer anything that I read in the books, no longer to accept blindly anything that had settled in my imagination, but rather to start each time from the beginning—to find the meaning in the words and music as if they had never before been "interpreted." I call this "taking things literally." And it is the music in particular that must be taken literally.

In the case of *The Magic Flute,* taking things literally forces us irrefutably to recognize the first aria of the queen as hypocrisy: this woman does not love her daughter, she slanders Sarastro, and she wants to use Tamino as a tool. She "performs" motherly grief, and actually offers her daughter as bait to any man who will help her to acquire the "sun circle," the pinnacle of power. She is a procuress. Once this has been recognized, the difficulties of interpreting Sarastro's character take care of themselves. He is not a king; he is the head of a fraternal order. It is his idea to unite Tamino, the heir of the neighboring realm, with Pamina, the daughter of the deceased king, in order to give his own country a new king and to join the two kingdoms together. In doing so he is executing the testament of the old king, who had given him the sun circle to prevent its possession by the power-hungry queen. And it enables him to extend the power of his order to a second kingdom.

What kind of a fraternity was it? We had always been told that

Mozart and Schikaneder had been guided here by Masonic ideas. This may be so, but at the time the work was written every educated man in Vienna was a Freemason; it was the thing to do. When you examine the libretto of *The Magic Flute* carefully, you will find in it more revolutionary than Masonic undertones. The fraternity forbids the acceptance of princes and crowned heads. And Sarastro, who conceived his grand plan perhaps as a result of long talks with the singular old king—a king who went into the wilderness and carved flutes out of ancient oak trees—must use pressure to arrange for the initiation of Tamino. This is not mythology; it is politics. The so-called fairy tale has turned into an exciting scenario. What a marvelous work, and what a pleasure to stage it!

Not only bad interpretations can distort a work to the point of being unrecognizable but similarly, and to an even greater extent, bad translations. Many translators of our most popular operas were completely devoid of any sense of responsibility. They made no effort to understand either the text or the action of the libretto. Their main concern was to construct German rhymes in the cloying style of nineteenth-century family magazines. To us the translation sounds unbearable, and besides, it is usually a mass of errors. Smetana's *Bartered Bride* is a perfect example.

I had put the opera into the repertory because I had a soprano in the ensemble who seemed predestined for the role of Mařenka. Before leaving to fulfill a guest engagement I decided on the cast. Immediately upon my return the rehearsals were to begin. As usual, I returned slightly later than anticipated, and time was of the essence. We are going to start in three days, I said. I anticipated no trouble; this was an opera full of vitality and gaiety. For two days we rehearsed the opening chorus and the aria of Mařenka. I became more and more depressed. I could not get past the stage when I like something quite well, and nothing more. But it is not enough for me to like something well. If the work does not take hold of me to the extent that I can no longer stop, then something is wrong. In *The Bartered Bride* I did not feel this compelling factor. I kept asking myself: what do these people want who sing in the beginning, what makes them so happy? Certainly the music is far more powerful than the words. This cannot be meaningless gaiety. I interrupted the rehearsals, and I asked the Czech Embassy to find someone for me who would agree to translate the entire text of *The Bartered Bride* within forty-eight hours. Naturally it would be an unpolished translation but it had to be absolutely literal. They found a student who furnished the translation within two days. When I saw it I almost fell from my chair. This was incredible.

One example. In the traditional German translation Mařenka sings, "Gläubig blick ich auf zu dir" (Devotedly I look up to you). This has been preceded by a recitative in which we learn that she suspects Jenik of being in love with another girl, since he refuses to tell her his name. What she really sings in this: "If I should ever find this out, I could never forgive you." I have softened it somewhat; in Czech it is even harder: "My bloodthirsty vengeance would pursue you." How genuinely Slavic! And this reads in our translation, "Devotedly I look up to you." It is a crime!

It was evening when the student brought the rough translation to me. A rehearsal was scheduled for the next morning. I canceled it. But I could not wait until I had retranslated the entire opera. The rehearsals were resumed. For three weeks I worked on the translation after every rehearsal, a Czech dictionary by my side. I tried to find the correct words for Smetana's rhythms. The results of my work went to the theater piecemeal and were mimeographed immediately. The soprano for whose sake I had scheduled the opera left us; she was not ready to give up the sentimental Mařenka that she had been used to. It broke her heart to know that everything was to be different. We found a new Mařenka. More than that: we discovered a new opera.

There is another point to the story. Several years after the premiere of *The Bartered Bride,* which turned out to be one of the greatest successes of the Komische Opera—more than a hundred performances—I engaged an outstanding conductor for the production of *The Sly Little Vixen* by Janáček. Vaclav Neumann, who loves *The Bartered Bride* above everything, went to attend a performance and felt, as did a number of other Czech nationals, partly overwhelmed and partly alienated. "The aria of Mařenka," he said, "is too harsh for me. After all, this is an idyll." And that was said by a Czech! *The Bartered Bride* is a national treasure; every Czech child sings the melodies, and they are sung in Czech in the same false spirit as that of the German translator—as "pretty tunes." At all costs, we must avoid excitement. Anyway, who takes opera seriously? Culinary opera.*

I do not know what happened at the world premiere of this opera. Perhaps Smetana felt as Verdi did after the premiere of *Ballo in Maschera.* You know Verdi's reaction from his letters. He went home in a fit of anger and demanded that the production be taken out of the repertory. "They distorted everything." Why? Because theater must be pleasant and comfortable, so that we can enjoy our chocolates while watching a performance.

During the period I am preparing to stage a work, taking it literally, I feel a mounting sense of urgency to see it in its setting, to transmit it into a definite, dramatic place of action—in other words, to bring the setting into my projection. Therefore the first collaborator I consult—after the conductor of course, who is present at the first piano reading—is the set designer. I cannot attend a musical rehearsal, much less start rehearsing myself, unless I know exactly what the set is going to look like. I loathe the "decorated" stage. This is what I mean by a "beautiful picture" with a "charming atmosphere." A decorated set does not act. It merely serves as culinary enjoyment. It accompanies the work instead of containing it. The stage set must hold everything necessary for the content and the dramatic structure of a scene.

*The terms "culinary art" and "culinary theater" were probably coined by Bertolt Brecht, to describe an irrelevant kind of entertainment that leaves the spectator pleased but uninvolved. Ed.

Naturally, the atmosphere or the style may be part of this, but only insofar as it actively contributes to the impression we are trying to create. What goes beyond that I call "decorated."

In order to work with the stage designer, I must know what happens in an act and how it happens. I have no preconceptions. The only respect in which I am ahead of him is the knowledge of the work, taken literally. This I must impart to him. Then we begin to discuss the totality of the style. The first question: where does the piece take place? This is the pivotal problem. The musical drama must find its world. It must be settled in a definite space which becomes its world. Again it is necessary to push aside prejudices and conventions. For that reason we seek answers that are as simple and clear as possible.

The second question: does it play on the stage of the Komische Oper or do we have to build within that stage another stage on which it takes place? *Fledermaus* played in our theater; we simply extended the style of the auditorium to the stage. On the other hand, *The Wise Maiden* by Orff does not play in our theater; it plays in the country, at a fair. So we spread out wooden planks on which we fastened big rough wooden posts; these were tied with ropes, and on the ropes coarse pieces of cloth were hung. All this took place on an exaggeratedly slanted stage, completely bare, no curtain—almost a Shakespearean stage.*

Carmen and *Der Freischütz* naturally also do not play in this theater. In *The Tales of Hoffmann,* however, we put a black portal in the style of Schinkel** in front of the stage, which could in this

*Particularly in older theaters, which often have a distinct architectural expression of their own, it is shortsighted of the designer to overlook this approach; an ultra-expressionistic set for *Wozzeck* will hardly play well when it tries to blend into a baroque theater space. Perhaps this is part of the reason for the enormous success of such operas as *Figaro* and *Cosi* at the Cuvilliès Theater in Munich or the Redoutensaal in Vienna.

**Karl Friedrich Schinkel (1781–1841) was a famous German painter and architect. He designed the theater in Berlin which is now known as the Deutsche Staatsoper and which after its destruction during World War II was rebuilt in its original form. His stage designs for *The Magic Flute* are still mentioned with much respect. Ed.

way be sharply separated from the auditorium. But behind the black portal we allowed the architecture of the auditorium to appear again, in the shape of several gaslit candelabra. In this fashion we deliberately blended the realistic impression, made possible by the sharp separation from the stage, with an element of fantasy.

Solutions of this kind do not simply exist. They originate from contact with the stage designer, who sketches while I explain, using his talent to transpose into the visual what I have found by studying the work, by taking it literally. At the same time he is the first testing ground of my conclusions. I expect him to start work entirely without prejudice. It is impossible for him to have formed certain pictorial conceptions; after all, he is not yet familiar with my interpretation. Along these lines, I would like to say that the use of famous painters as set designers, which is particularly popular with the French, is not only wrong but even grotesque. What it produces can only be a picture gallery. The set designer must be above all a gifted painter, even more so than a gifted architect, but he must give himself utterly to the stage if he is to explore and master the laws of the stage, which are so radically different from those of painting. He helps me with his pictorial imagination. I am ready to listen to his suggestions to the point of compromising with my own ideas.* We try them out immediately to test their intelligibility, which always remains the most powerful motivation in my work. I must be able to take for granted the active interest of my collaborator—the same active interest that I like to stir up in the audience. Naturally, I know very well what I want to do, but at this stage I insist on everything remaining open and subject to correction.

For that reason I do not settle on the ground plan until I have reached an agreement with the designer about the set. As a young stage director I used to do it the other way around: the designer

*Felsenstein uses the word *Charakterlosigkeit* (lack of character, spinelessness) which in this context stubbornly resists translation. Ed.

had to accept my instructions for the ground plan, which had been worked out to the tiniest detail. Now, after so many years of experience, I know that this is wrong. The ground plan is contained in the libretto and the score; while the set is being designed it comes into existence all by itself; it merely takes a little time to come to the surface, since it is the result of a process of clarification.

I have to admit that exceptions are possible. When I staged *The Magic Flute,* it was clear to me that the opera had to be set within the framework of a baroque theater. I knew that into this frame, which was to be fashioned in a style derived from great historical patterns, no complete sets could be built. Hints would have to suffice, always the necessary motifs, with a drop in back of them merely to show whether the scene was played inside or outside. I also knew that the Egyptian theme, the conventional pyramid style, had no business in this opera. This was the conclusion I reached by taking the libretto literally. yet only the designer, Rudolf Heinrich, found the style in which the fairy tale within the baroque frame could be expressed most naturally: Persian miniatures, East Indian shapes, the Orient.

When I ask myself why after so many years I still have not given up my work, which never seems to produce unmixed results, there is only one answer: driving me and urging me on to further efforts is my inborn hope that it might be possible, at least temporarily, to eliminate the flatness of repetition, and to convey to the spectators a human, a primeval expression of feeling in which they may recognize their own longings and desires.

Modern man has lost touch with his beginnings. He is frozen in a civilization that is devoid of mystery. Yet there is a vague longing still left within him, and this longing can be fulfilled in art. When in the theater he experiences re-creation of the primitive, he rediscovers the primitive within himself. This is the only possible interpretation of the theater's humanistic task. "Human" is not identical with "primitive," but it is no longer human when the primitive is not contained in it. This is undoubtedly what Brecht meant when in his late years he characterized naïveté* as the highest of all aesthetic categories.

The primitive is not an uncontrollable drive to expression. If on one hand singing cannot come into existence until everyday sobriety is pushed aside and the desire for heightened expression becomes overwhelming, it can on the other hand never come into existence without being rendered into form: the need for expression is paired with the need for creative form. On the stage, singing is generated with the greatest difficulty when the partners are forced to exchange dry statements without emotion. An aria is much easier to realize, both vocally and dramatically. Usually it is preceded by a recitative containing dramatic tension, and then the point is reached where the emotion stands still, as it were, and urges toward vocal expression. The sung dialogue, however, must no less give the audience the impression that the actors *must* sing, that speaking as a means of expression is no longer sufficient, that something primitive breaks out and blends with the dialogue. The great masters of sung drama knew this well and considered it carefully. Even in the most artful duet the intensification into the primitive is included, and this alone makes singing on stage possible.

There is one example of the way an entire work, written as a spoken play, from the very first moment was forced into music: Verdi's *Otello.* Verdi and the librettist Boito omitted the first act of the Shakespearean drama, thereby making room for music. A new exposition was created: unchained powers of nature, thunder and lightning, storm, the roaring sea, chaos. Out there the battle is raging. Everybody knows what depends on its outcome. The crowd trembles for the fleet, trembles for Cyprus, trembles for Venice. Boito and Verdi have heightened the situation until it touches elemental nature itself. The cosmic power of this new beginning must release the furioso of the singing and out of this tempestuousness the human being Otello is hurled into the ac-

*In the sense of ultimate simplicity, without preconceived ideas.

tion. After the victorious battle he finds at last, and perhaps for the first time, fulfillment of his dreams of happiness and peace. Otello's sorrow-filled life and Desdemona's love and understanding are fused into a situation in which two people *must* sing, "driven by love."

This is the origin of singing on the stage.

Work with the singer starts with my giving him information on the background of the piece. Sometimes we sit opposite each other for two hours and only talk. At other times there are three or four of us—there may be the conductor, or the assistant conductor, or the set designer. This applies particularly to the early stages, as long as it is important to familiarize as many participants as possible with the information I have gathered. I know the characters. I know what they do and how they behave when they are not on stage, in scenes that have not been written; I have investigated their earlier lives, their private lives. That information must be imparted to the singers and to my collaborators.

Let us take the role of Tamino. I have given the singer the necessary information. Now I ask him to sing his aria, which starts with the words "Dies Bildnis ist bezaubernd schön" (This portrait is bewitchingly beautiful).* He tends to sing it in the fashion to which he is accustomed: merely striving for beauty and lyricism. I try to explain to him that finding something beautiful is not nearly enough reason to sing. Nor is it right for him simply to state his opinion of the portrait; that would be no reason for singing either.

What has happened? The First Lady, who strikes him as rather importunate, has pressed an object into his hand that he has accepted only because it has come from the queen, whom he greatly admires. Thus he has taken the portrait almost reluc-

*The words used here (my own) are an absolutely literal translation, in order to render the exact psychological meaning of the sentence. No one should attempt to sing them; they do not fit. Ed.

tantly. And now, when in spite of this reluctance he decides to look at it, a miracle happens; he is overwhelmed by something he has never before experienced: he loves for the first time—not because the girl depicted in the portrait is beautiful, but because fate has caused lightning to strike him. His exclamation, "This portrait is bewitchingly beautiful," bursts forth from him as if a valve had opened.

Mozart wanted it that way. The notes cannot be sung in any other fashion. Two bars of the orchestra with E♭ major chords. Then the singer attacks in a devilishly difficult tessitura. He starts with the B♭ right below middle C, and he must sing up to the G; this is very hard. However, if he tries to feel the B♭ one octave higher, and furthermore to imagine the E♭ of the second octave above middle C—not to sing it, merely to imagine it while the orchestra plays the two measures—then the actual B♭ lies far below the imagined high E♭ and he can sing down to the G. When he first looks at the portrait and lightning strikes him, he finds himself on the high E♭ of excitement.

The activity of concentration transports the singer into a state of sublimity. It increases in the downward glide to the next phrase. The singer now begins to sense that the orchestral accompaniment is at least as important to him as the singing itself, for Tamino's entire character is contained in it: the aria is a character portrait. He is filled with an irresistible urge to know what has happened to him. (Later, during the trials, this asserts itself very clearly and here it manifests itself as the need to find out.) He has never experienced such great love and he is groping for an explanation.

After this, two or three days will pass until the singer is ready, physically and mentally, to study the aria on the basis of all this. We rehearse with him together, the assistant conductor and I, until we feel that he has reached the necessary state. If for any reason he does not live up to expectations, we can still put someone else in his place.

The most difficult task always is to get the singer to the point of being able to create the expression out of his own inner concentration. In order to prevent misunderstandings let me say that I would find it just as repulsive as Brecht did if the singer were to stop here. But in contrast to Brecht, at least to the theorist Brecht, I maintain that the actor can create the necessary psychological state only by the means that he himself possesses, that is, by his own feelings, his nerves, his individuality.* He must utilize his entire psyche in the role. His innermost feelings must be in continuous and unbreakable contact with the feelings of the human being that he has to create. The exclusion of private emotion, the sensitivity and excitability, from the work of an actor renders him impotent, whether he is supposed to express emotions or to "alienate" them.

Incidentally, in the music theater all this is far more difficult than in the drama. There I can use the help of pauses or of varying interpretations of the text. Here it is necessary to feel my way into the core of an unchangeable musical score as if I myself had written it.

I had allowed the singer portraying Tamino to begin with the first-act aria, since it is his most important test. If during the course of the first few rehearsals he has proved that he can handle the aria, then I must insist that we now proceed chronologically. The drama can be developed only through the development of the role. Therefore we must now go back to the beginning. And this beginning, God knows, is no easy matter. Why does Tamino faint? He is a brave young man, a superbly skilled hunter. He has shot off all his arrows. It is hard to believe that he should not have hit the target. He is courageous, a sportsman, but something monstrous has happened to him: he has found the snake to be invulnerable. This so fascinates him that he cannot detach himself. He wants to flee, but at the same time he is rooted to the side

*The author alludes here to Brecht's well-known opinion that it is the actor's task to create an intensity without himself becoming part of it, a process usually referred to as "alienation." Ed.

of the reptile. His youthful fighting spirit is paralyzed by something incomprehensible. This entire inner process, exactly composed by Mozart, results in overexertion, which drains the blood from his head. That explains the fainting.

Once someone can act the beginning correctly, he should find no more problems in the entire role. Most of all, this will show what I call "inner tempo." The ability to sense and assimilate a work's metric tempo is a decisive factor for a singer. By metric tempo I mean the subdivision of a phrase or of a measure into the smallest rhythmic value occurring in that measure, as it relates to the emotional and spiritual presentation. Take again, for instance, the beginning, "Zu Hilfe, zu Hilfe, sonst bin ich verloren!" (Help, help, or I'm lost!) If I work with an eminently gifted singer I make him sing this in sixteenth notes, but I might even be satisfied if he can manage it in eighths. That is the "inner tempo." If he bases his acting on this, if he looks for a bush behind which he can hide, then it must be possible to feel the eighths. If he looks around "in quarters" then I interrupt.

It is by no means a question of making the notes or the rhythms themselves perceptible through acting. Once the singer grasps the inner tempo and makes it his own, the action follows without difficulty; he no longer copies the music; rather, he is imbued with it to such an extent that he moves in eighth notes.*

Whether we try to absorb the content of a scene by using exercises and auxiliary devices, or whether we employ obvious realistic analogies, it comes to the same thing: music, in the orchestra as well as in singing, must not for one single second become less than compelling. You cannot sing the above passage in the manner described and you should not even try. But you must understand it in this way. You must recognize its truth. In

*Lest there be a misunderstanding: let no one assume that Felsenstein is trying to turn the tenor into a half-insane grasshopper, swirling around in sixteenth notes! This imaginary rhythm never shows as a rhythm, only as an intensity. It keeps the singing actor from becoming indifferent, and it lends cohesion to his interpretation. Ed.

Mozart's works—not only in *The Magic Flute* but also in *Figaro* and *Don Giovanni*—every measure and every note is truth. I would even call them programmed. I know that a number of music critics will not subscribe to this: they feel that everything is beautiful sound and rhythm and are annoyed when music becomes specific. I am annoyed when this is accomplished so awkwardly that I as a listener am made to feel stupid; just the same, it must become specific because the composer wrote it as that.

Perhaps someone will ask: what then do the strophic repeats in the numbers mean? Dramatically speaking, I say, there is no repetition. What appears as a repetition in the musical form affects us differently on the stage; simply because one strophe follows the other, the second can no longer be the same as the first, since it relates to it. When a great dramatic composer puts in a repeat, this may mean, for example, that the character was not understood the first time. Or the verses may represent different gradations, as in the song of Papageno, who presents himself and tries to look important, and in each succeeding verse reaffirms his hunger for love more strongly.

It is always a happy experience for me when a singing actor appears more and more at ease in his role, as he succeeds in assimilating completely and precisely everything that I call program, meaning the truth in the music. Suddenly he feels, sings, and "plays" the notes as if he had written them himself. At the peak of necessity the musician in him becomes liberated. In that moment, in a rehearsal or during a performance, he discovers within himself the capacity to *compose* the opera in the way intended by Mozart or Verdi. What happens then between him and the conductor—if the conductor is ready to go along—is a miracle, one of the most beautiful experiences imaginable. It is perfect music theater.

Time and again the music plays the decisive role. When I stage a work, I make music with my singers. Music and singing must be recognized in their dramatic function; that is called music theater. To fashion music-making and singing on the stage into a credible, convincing, and absolutely essential human statement: this must always be the primary task.

Professor Walter Felsenstein, Intendant of the Komische Oper, Berlin, during rehearsal.

The Magic Flute, MOZART
(set and costumes: Rudolf Heinrich)

Scene with Tamino (Manfred Hopp) and the Three Boys

Scene with Pamina (Elisabeth Ebert), Sarastro (Herbert Rössler), and chorus

La Traviata, Verdi

(set and costumes: Rudolf Heinrich)

Scene with Violetta (Melitta Muszely) and Alfredo (John Moulson)

The Adventures of Háry János, KODÁLY

(musical direction: Geza Oberfrank
staging: Walter Felsenstein
set: Reinhart Zimmermann
costumes: Eleanore Kleiber)

Prologue

First Adventure. Left to right: Örzse (Jana Smitkova), Háry János (Siegfried Vogel), Marczi (Rudolf Asmus), Marie-Louise (Ingrid Czerny), Baron von Ebelasztin (Helmut Polze)

Third Adventure. Háry János (Siegfried Vogel) and Napoleon (Frank Folker)

Fourth Adventure. Empress (Irmgard Arnold) and Marie-Louise (Ingrid Czerny)

Don Giovanni, MOZART

(set: Reinhart Zimmermann
costumes: Sylta-Marie Busse)

Scene with Don Ottavio (Otto Rogge) and Donna Anna (Christa Noack)

A Midsummer Night's Dream, BRITTEN
(set and costumes: Rudolf Heinrich)

Scene with Bottom (Rudolf Asmus) and Titania (Bernadine Oliphant)

Scene with Flute (Werner Enders), Snout (Frank Folker), and Bottom (Rudolf Asmus)

Carmen, Bizet

Micaela (Galina Pissarenko)

Act One: Chorus

(On facing page from top to bottom)

Act One: Carmen (Emma Sarkissjan) and José (Günter Weismann)

Act Two: Carmen (Emma Sarkissjan) and José (W. Ossipow)

Act Four: Carmen (Emma Sarkissjan) and José (Günter Weismann)

Tales of Hoffman, OFFENBACH
(set and costumes: Rudolf Heinrich)

Scene with Hoffmann (John Moulson) and chorus

The Love of Three Oranges, PROKOFIEV
(set: Valeri Lewental
costumes: Marina Sokolowa)

Scene with Ninetta (Ingrid Czerny) and the Prince (Hans-Otto Rogge)

Bluebeard, OFFENBACH
(set and costumes: Wilfred Werz)

Scene with Clementine (Ruth Schob-Lipka), King Bobeche (Werner Enders), Hermia (Ingrid Czerny), and Saphir (Manfred Hopp)

Scene with Bluebeard (Hanns Nocker) and others

Scene with Bluebeard (Hanns Nocker) and Boulotte (Anny Schlemm)

Scene with Boulotte (Anny Schlemm) and Popolani (Rudolf Asmus)

Fiddler on the Roof, STEIN/BOCK/HARNICK
(set: Valeri Lewental
costumes: Marina Sokolowa)

Professor Felsenstein rehearsing with Rudolf Asmus

Scene with Zeitel (Friederike Wulff-Apelt), Motel (Werner Enders), and the Rabbi (Eberhard Valentin)

Fifth scene with Rudolf Asmus

Sixteenth scene with Rudolf Asmus, Frank Folker, Irmgard Arnold, Friederike Wulff-Apelt, Frieder Euler, and Werner Enders.

PART TWO

Felsenstein on Specific Problems

Background investigations and explanations by Felsenstein on some of the works that he has staged, and on his technique of staging them

7

Why Does Pamina Flee?

(Rehearsal discussion for the first Pamina scene with students of the Bayreuth master classes, 1960)

FELSENSTEIN: Even scholarly books on music history perpetuate the absurdity that *The Magic Flute* is a potboiler by Schikaneder, the theater manager, which is elevated only by Mozart's magnificent music. I could prove to you that Schikaneder's work is in itself outstanding; combined with Mozart's music, it was in its own time a revolutionary, even dangerous declaration, notwithstanding its appearance, or rather disguise, as a fairy tale.

STUDENT: Is it not true that the Queen of the Night is a benevolent character in the first half of the work but that in the second half she becomes evil and dangerous? And is not exactly the reverse true of Monostatos?

FELSENSTEIN: You are repeating precisely what is in the music history books. But it is wrong, as a number of authorities have proved recently. There is no "break" between the first and second acts. Let me explain this.

The opinion that the Queen of the Night is benevolent in her first aria rests mainly on the fact that this aria is misinterpreted by many singers. In actuality it represents a scheming, hypocritical disguise. The queen acts the role of a mournful, affectionate mother in order to win Tamino to her side.

STUDENT: How do you explain the three ladies, who at first persuade Tamino to liberate Pamina but later try to prevent him from accomplishing his purpose?

FELSENSTEIN: The ladies do not carry out the queen's order at all; instead, they compete with each other to possess Tamino themselves. But in the second act when they try to hinder Tamino, they are acting exactly in accord with the queen's wishes.

The drama uses as its main theme the fight over the sun circle, which in the fairy tale of *The Magic Flute* makes people all-powerful. It would correspond in any other century with any device of power politics. The lying machinations and seductive trickery of the Queen of the Night and her followers are part of the battle for the powerful sun circle, and so are the countermeasures of the group around Sarastro.

However, for the moment let us limit ourselves to the initial situation, the background of Pamina's first scene. (To the singer): When you first appear as Pamina, where do you come from?

SINGER: I am a prisoner of Sarastro, I have fled, and Monostatos has caught me again.

FELSENSTEIN: Why did you flee?

SINGER: I wanted to return to my mother.

FELSENSTEIN: No. Why did you flee from Monostatos?

QUESTION FROM THE AUDIENCE: Did she really flee from Monostatos, not from Sarastro?

FELSENSTEIN: It is good that you brought this up. It shows that I shall have to go back a little further. How long has Pamina actually been in Sarastro's custody? This is not specified. Anything that I am going to say about it, however, is not my own conception; it comes clearly and directly out of the play itself. To justify and motivate all details of Pamina's life at Sarastro's court, you have to assume that she has been there for at least one and a half or two years. The Queen of the Night tells Tamino in her first aria that Sarastro carried Pamina away by force. The queen's account of it leads us to believe that Sarastro is a bandit, a violent criminal. Much later, at the end of the first act, we learn that Sarastro actually did abduct Pamina, but only in the beginning of the second act does it become clear why he did it. In order to pinpoint Pamina's situation, which for the spectator only gradually falls into place, I shall again have to go back a little further.

The actress who portrays Pamina must understand precisely Pamina's relationship with her father. We know that the father, who is no longer living, was the ruler of a great kingdom. Within the same kingdom we also find the fraternal order of the Initiates. This fact in itself hides the root of a conflict: the humanistic doctrine of the brotherhood of all mankind, for which the order stands, cannot be reconciled with the idea of royal domination. It obviously follows that the order has a policy of suspicion toward any member of the ruling class. The order, according to my estimate, has about two thousand members; I assume this because Mozart and Schikaneder specify that the senate of the order consists of eighteen leaders.

Another difficulty arises directly from Sarastro himself. He is still relatively young, and never before in the history of the order have the Initiates been ruled by so young a sovereign. It is even less to the liking of the order that Sarastro had been an intimate friend of the ruling king. Furthermore, the queen had been infuriated by the friendship. For she is, as the text distinctly indicates, extremely hungry for power. Therefore she is understandably prejudiced against Sarastro, and is also suspicious, because the talks between her husband and Sarastro had always taken place in private, without her. The king loved his wife deeply; she is a very beautiful woman. And from the plot of the play, which starts after the death of the king, we infer that he was completely under her influence. Evidently the queen's feeling for her husband was not as strong as his for her, but she loved his power. In spite of his great love the king realized, from his wife's craving for power and from many things she said, that it might be a disaster for the entire country if the sun circle were to fall into the queen's hands after his death.

From your astonished expressions I assume that you suspect me of offering you my own interpretation. Actually, I am analyzing the contents of *The Magic Flute.*

STUDENT: And you are following Schikaneder's libretto?

FELSENSTEIN: Naturally.

STUDENT: Actually, you are analyzing not Schikaneder but Schikaneder-Mozart?

FELSENSTEIN: Of course.

STUDENT: As we know *The Magic Flute* today, there is no reference to the king in either the words or the music.

FELSENSTEIN: Parts of the dialogue are often omitted in performance, but there are several references to Pamina's father. For example, Pamina tells in the beginning of the trials by fire and water how the flute came into existence, and mentions her father:

Es schnitt in einer Zauberstunde
Mein Vater sie aus tiefstem Grunde
der tausendjähr'gen Eiche aus.
(In a magic hour my father cut it
out of the bottom of the
thousand-year-old oak tree)

This portion is never cut. Let us continue. As the king believed that the sun circle in the hands of his wife would become a tremendous danger to humanity, since through its power she could subjugate other countries or even conquer the world, he gave it to the Initiates, unbeknown to his wife or to Pamina. In a scene between the queen and Pamina, immediately preceding the queen's second aria—a passage that is often cut—the queen tells Pamina in greatest excitement how she learned from her husband only in his last hour about the presentation of the sun circle to the Initiates. This hour was filled with a bitter struggle between him and the queen to have him revoke his testament, the gift to Sarastro. It is probable that the king, in his boundless love for his wife, was not always strong enough to oppose her, but he was inflexible in this case.

If we do not accept this background and these relationships as basic to the plot, then the role of the queen, and even that of Sarastro, can never be correctly interpreted. This usually makes no difference to opera lovers; to them the Queen of the Night is simply a coloratura soprano who need not worry about anything except her coloraturas.

I am not betraying any secret when I say that a coloratura soprano is really not capable of interpreting the role of the queen. If you study the score, you will see for yourselves that it must be sung by a dramatic soprano.*

Let me go on. The king was fully aware that when his wife learned the sun circle had been given away she would not rest for a moment until she had regained possession of it, even at the cost of armed intervention. Therefore when he gave it to his friend Sarastro, he asked him to take Pamina into his custody for the first years after the king's death. This would save her from the disastrous influence of her mother, who would use any means to fight for power. Thus Sarastro, in order to carry out his friend's last wish, must allow himself to be suspected of being a criminal.

Pamina had to be removed from the influence of her mother. This does not indicate that she does not fervently love her

*Perhaps we ought to be more explicit in categorizing and ask for a dramatic coloratura. Ed.

mother—on the contrary! But we must also assume that Pamina was particularly close to her father. This we learn from her narrative: she was a witness when her father carved the magic flute [see quotation above].

STUDENT: Is the quotation a reference to an actual "magic" hour?

FELSENSTEIN: Yes, a certain astrological hour. The fact that the flute became not just a toy but the magic flute could be assured only by a particular constellation of the stars.

STUDENT: From the quotation it is not evident, though, that Pamina was present when the magic flute was carved.

FELSENSTEIN: Then how did she learn about it?

STUDENT: From her mother.

FELSENSTEIN: The queen did not tell Pamina anything about it. In any case, the story of the magic flute is one of the secrets of the king's realm. Perhaps it would not be too easy for the inhabitants of the state to understand why their ruler spends his time carving flutes. Therefore Pamina could not have been told about it either, not by her mother and not by a third person. Furthermore, even the three ladies do not know the story of the magic flute they give to Tamino: would that not have spoiled the mystery of the flute? The ladies deliver the present; only on that day does the queen say, "This is the flute that affords its owner absolute protection."

But there is a still better justification for our assumption. Tamino is facing an ordeal which may mean death, the trials by fire and water, but he is doing it of his own free will. Is it not extremely unlikely that at such a time Pamina should start telling fairy tales? She does exactly the opposite. She does what is plausible and right. At a time when both of them, in spite of their courage and their will to live, fear destruction by fire or water—at this time she recalls instinctively the significance of the flute. It had never occurred to her until now, but in this moment of utter concentration she remembers what her father told her long ago when he carved the flute. Otherwise, the scene between Pamina and Tamino before the trials would merely be filled with small talk. That, however, is unthinkable, in view of the music.

Pamina, for reasons that are already known to us, is being treated at the court of Sarastro as if she were a princess of his own household, except that she is not allowed to leave the palace. But even the best treatment cannot prevent her from being homesick for her mother. The feelings of being abandoned and of homesickness are particularly strong in her, since obviously she is unable to understand the behavior of the people around her. In fact, the attention she receives is an embarrassment. Not that Pamina is prudish. She is a beautiful, inexperienced girl who is not aware that she was born to be loved. This fact is especially important, because an innocent girl totally directed toward love, even if subconsciously, is not prudish. I am referring to what the bourgeois world, in its own lack of innocence, calls "immoral" or "sinful." Since a really innocent girl does not know what is meant by "sin," she cannot display modesty in the ordinary sense. But this is significant. Pamina is not a nun; she is a passionate girl who has never loved a man. She has a great destiny: like a star, she has come into the world for Tamino (only she does not know it). Even if she had not met Tamino at this time, she would probably wait for him to her dying day—without being prudish.

Through this facet of Pamina's character we must understand her relationship with Sarastro. The most cogent proof of the inner bond between the two is found at the end of the first Act, although it is well concealed. Here, in front of everybody, Sarastro speaks about Pamina and himself. And even though the scene is quite short, Mozart surprisingly leaves so much time for the sentence "Du liebest einen andern sehr" (You love someone else very much) that he has it repeated in the orchestra as well as in the text.

Sarastro cannot say any more at this moment, since there are other people present. But Pamina understands him very well, which makes her even more nervous.

Let us now try to project this same action back to the starting point, to the beginning of our scene. Clearly we cannot say that Pamina flees from Sarastro, even though she is afraid of him to some extent. The underlying reasons for her attempt to flee are complex, but the immediate cause for it is Monostatos.

8

Donna Anna and Don Giovanni

(From the program booklet of the Komische Oper on the day of the premiere performance, December 4, 1966)

What happened in Donna Anna's room between her and Don Giovanni?

The experts differ widely on this point. Mozart and Da Ponte do not furnish any direct information, undoubtedly in order to force the spectator to find the answer in the behavior of the characters themselves. This is not easy, and if the acting is inadequate, it is quite impossible. But a careful, faithful interpretation on one side of the footlights, and proper attention on the other, should accomplish what the creators wished. A thorough study of the scenes between Anna, Giovanni, and Ottavio (of the words, of course, but primarily of the music) may bring an understanding that will not merely clarify the mysterious background of the drama; it will also help to pinpoint the incident immediately preceding the beginning of the opera as a point of departure for almost all of Giovanni's behavior. Thus the tragedy of Donna Anna will become completely comprehensible.

The assumption that Giovanni possessed Anna presupposes either that she gave herself to the strange intruder or that she was raped by him. That the former could not have happened requires no explanation. On the other hand, a rape would be completely at variance with Giovanni's personality and principles. His desire grows out of an infinite sensual craving; it idealizes the victim of the moment and transforms her into the requisite state. Confronted by him, the woman feels herself lifted out of reality and responds to his desire with a passion that is forever unforgettable. This magic of Giovanni is totally irresistible and he takes great joy in it, but it contains an unending need for intensification, variation, and completion which knows no moral sense, conquers all resistance, and is impervious to all reason.

Furthermore, if Giovanni had attained the aim of his desire with Anna, why does he not take flight to thwart her dangerous attempt to disclose his identity? Why does he—the highly respected grandee, friend of the Commendatore and of Ottavio, whose conduct is not known to anyone in Seville except Leporello—why does he expose himself to the danger of being recognized? How does the relatively extended duet (or trio, actually) in the first scene make sense unless we see that Giovanni, who has never encountered resistance from a woman, cannot understand Anna's behavior? Incapable of admitting defeat, he believes that he can overcome Anna's hostility; unruffled by the thought that the nocturnal turmoil must unavoidably bring forth witnesses, he lets himself be challenged to a duel and so comes to stab the Commendatore, who is his friend and Anna's father. He, the master of every situation, who until now has lived only according to his will and his desire, is no longer able to control his own fate. The end of Don Giovanni has begun.

If Giovanni was unable to seduce Anna, does then her narrative (recitative, no. 10)* tell the whole story of what happened between her and Giovanni? When she calls upon her fiancé to save her father, why does she not tell him the reason for the duel—her encounter with the stranger in her bedroom? She allows Ottavio to vow revenge for her father's death but not yet for the violation of her maidenly honor. Her extremely alarming state at

*In the Peters edition.

this time leads us to assume that Ottavio will visit her again early in the morning, and probably will not leave her until the meeting with Giovanni in the afternoon.*

Only now, when she has recognized in Giovanni the visitor of the previous night, which might not have happened so soon if she had not encountered Elvira—only now does she tell Ottavio the happenings of the night before, in a fashion which makes it clear to us that the experience with Giovanni has upset her no less than her father's death. Only now does she demand revenge on the man "chi l'onore rapire a me volse" (who wanted to rob me of my honor).

Is she lying to Ottavio?

Of that she is hardly capable. I am convinced that no word in her narrative is untrue. She limits her report to the facts, however, and does not reveal how the event affected her psychologically (at least not in words; Mozart tells us more). We must assume the daughter of the Commendatore to be a girl brought up in the strictness of Spanish-Catholic nobility. After the early loss of her mother she formed a very close relationship with her father. Ottavio is the first man whose deep, constant love she is able to return. The father also favors a union with this young nobleman, who in every respect is steadfast and aristocratic. After a suitably long engagement the marriage is now imminent.

In the eyes of Giovanni, Anna until now has been nothing more than the little daughter of the highly esteemed Commendatore (in whose good graces he wishes to remain for reasons of prestige) and more recently the fiancée of a devoted friend. Returning to Seville after a prolonged absence, and for once without a liaison, he suddenly sees the woman in Anna, and with an infalli-

*Since the times of day are not stated exactly in the libretto, they could be reconstructed as follows: nos. 3 and 4 in the morning after the fateful night; the ball in Giovanni's palace takes place the same evening. Since there is no interruption in time between the first encounter of Zerlina and Giovanni and the ball, one cannot assume an earlier time for the first chorus scene (no. 5) than the afternoon. (Footnote by the author)

ble instinct recognizes in her dormant possibilities of which she herself is totally unaware. Since in his identity as Don Giovanni she is inaccessible to him, he suddenly conceives the plan of entering her bedroom at night, masked and unrecognizable. This idea is absurd, in view of its danger and possible consequences; its adoption by the adventurer, who is so experienced and protective of himself, leads us to conclude that this time his passion, even according to his standards, must be extraordinary. He relies on the effect of his desire, and rightly so: Anna believes the figure suddenly appearing in the dark to be Ottavio. With her thoughts centered around the wedding, she does not resent the bold, illicit behavior of her fiancé in spite of her initial shock. She speaks to the man in surprised and tender words, but receives no reply. Silently he approaches her, coming closer and closer; the first touch makes her realize her error. But together with her horrified fear another feeling, unknown and enormous, seizes her, a feeling she is unable to resist: the natural-born sexual partner for Giovanni has come to life in her with a vehemence that is stronger than her conscious self. Her first scream is less a scream for help than an expression of being overwhelmed. "Who are you?" she gasps. The masked stranger silently holds her in his embrace. If he now revealed himself and claimed her for his own, there is no telling what might happen: the father, Ottavio, the marriage, all might be forgotten. Was this perhaps God's will? "Who are you?" "A man without a name," he answers (which is what he actually says in the play by Tirso de Molina). By now she has nearly lost her senses, but giving herself to a man who does not wish to be recognized—no, that is degradation; that would make her a harlot. The pride of generations erupts, and she engages Giovanni in a fight that forces him to leave the room. She follows, and her passionate excitement turns into hatred of the criminal. But her hatred cannot make her forget the transformation that has taken place within her.

Shamed and in desperate helplessness, she is unable to address her father and to keep him from fighting the duel with the stranger, who is evidently very powerful. She rushes off and comes back with Ottavio, but too late. The father is dead. When later, awakening from her fainting spell, she addresses Ottavio as a murderer, this proves that in her indescribable confusion she has forgotten Ottavio's presence; she is solely occupied with the stranger, with her feeling of guilt, and with the inescapability of her crisis. "Fuggi, crudele, fuggi, lascia che mora anch'io" (Flee, cruel one, let me also die) is the desperate scream of a woman who is near insanity, and it could also read, "Flee, and free me of your presence!" It is clear that she cannot confide in anyone now, least of all in Ottavio.

Giovanni can neither understand nor accept that his passionate desire is to remain unfulfilled. Since he lacks any experience even remotely comparable, this situation spells disaster for him. Only in this fashion can we explain the haste with which he, the master of amorous arts who is always sure of his success, now seeks self-affirmation in new adventures; the almost helpless insecurity which he experiences on meeting Elvira again; and also the cheap, thoughtless invitation of the peasant wedding congregation to his castle (this stupefies even Leporello) only for the purpose of being alone with Zerlina for a few moments. In Zerlina's enchantment and marvelous readiness he seems to find himself again. Then he is thrown into complete bewilderment by Elvira's aria (no. 8). But as soon as he meets Donna Anna, and in the hope that he will not be singled out as the nocturnal intruder, he deliberately offers his assistance to her. Even Elvira's renewed accusation (quartet, no. 9), which he vainly tries to refute with Anna and Ottavio, does not prevent him from expectantly inviting Anna (not Ottavio) to his castle. During the following scenes Giovanni concentrates exclusively on Zerlina. But when Anna stands before him without a mask—it is his last encounter with her—he addresses only her, in spite of being threatened by Ottavio and Elvira, with "Ah credete" (Ah believe me), in order to dissuade her from the belief that he was trying to seduce Zerlina.

From the manner in which Giovanni asks her to visit him (recitative following no. 9), Anna recognizes in the friend whom she was about to ask for help against the murderer of her father none other than the criminal himself. Her dismay, her desperate fury, and her outraged pride know no bounds. The fact that it was Giovanni who lusted for her, to whom she almost gave herself, and who had wanted to use her as he had used so many other women, merely to enhance his reputation—that is worse than everything else. Now Ottavio learns what he must know in order to avenge her honor. The way Mozart composed Anna's recognition of Giovanni, her narrative and her cry for vengeance, is dramatically superior to the Anna-Giovanni duet as well as to all the portions of the first scene surrounding the death of her father; it will serve to invalidate any claim that this interpretation of Anna's behavior is arbitrary.

That Anna herself has scruples concerning the implementation of the plan of vengeance and lets Elvira take the lead (trio of the "masks," first finale) only proves her inability to conquer the tremendous inner conflict. This also becomes clear from her "Io moro" (I am dying) during the minuet, when Elvira calls her attention to Giovanni's wooing of Zerlina. Pity, not fear, prevents Anna from confiding in Ottavio, to whom her unchanged faith is pledged with the betrothal and with her deep gratitude. But when she asks him to postpone the wedding for another year (last sextet), she knows that she will not live to the end of that year. Even before this, the aria no. 23 is permeated with a strange, otherworldly feeling: the Larghetto seems to be more a farewell than a pledge, and the Allegretto moderato is aglow with the hope of redemption. There is no doubt that death is in her thoughts.

It is generally known that Da Ponte based his libretto on Bertati's libretto for the opera of Gazzaniga, which was presented in Vienna shortly before the creation of Mozart's work. In that version Anna appears only in one brief episode. Since our study draws much more on the score than on the libretto, we may conclude that it was primarily Mozart's idea to counterbalance the drama of Elvira with Anna's tragedy.

9

On Janáček's Dramatic Works

(From a speech delivered at the Janáček Congress in Brno, Czechoslovakia, 1958)

Man is most alone in those experiences and feelings in which science and reason have no part and about which he cannot communicate in his language. It is the noblest task of art, and preponderantly of music, to liberate human beings from their loneliness in those areas, to bring them in contact with each other, and to give them belief in their community with others. Great and immortal masters have fulfilled this task, and have helped innumerable individuals to endure their existence. But no one until now has expressed the indescribable as directly, as immediately, as starkly and profoundly, as unmistakably, and as disconcertingly as Janáček. Where our immortal classics and some of the later masters find the musical metaphor for a great emotion in the movement of a symphony or in a scene from an opera, Janáček finds in a few measures the exact and merciless word for the inexpressible. Sometimes it seems as if in his handwriting music had become an entirely new means of human communication.

I think that Janáček's study of the word cadence in folksongs and of the audible utterances of all creatures—a study such as no musician had ever undertaken before him—is a unique manifestation of his love for life and of his compassion for other men. All this was acquired, was tried and tried again, in order to be able truly to communicate with all human beings, to intrude into their loneliness, and to help them discover that they are not completely alone. And for that reason I think the friends of Janáček ought to think carefully about how the master's testament can be made accessible to all men, since the dissemination of his work is still in its beginnings. This is first and foremost a question of interpretation. Any audience listening to Janáček's music for the first time is almost without exception unable to understand it, because for generations audiences have become accustomed to a more expansive type of musical communication. In older music as well as in the more recent, more time is allowed for the absorption of a musical expression, whether it is through the duration of a phrase or through its repetition. Janáček shows a terseness and concentration of communication which almost disregards an audience's receptivity and capability to absorb. Moreover, the larger part of the public is used to a pleasurable —a passive—reception of music. Janáček forces you to take cognizance of the content, because every sentence and every note represents a direct statement.

This means that the interpretation requires the utmost clarity and vividness, capturing the listener's attention at least to the extent that the desire is awakened in him to hear the work again and to get to know it better.

Clarity and vividness in staging a work by Janáček entail the most generally comprehensible representation of all that lies behind the words and the orchestral sounds—in other words, not a superficial staging that limits itself to the outer progression of the action, but a penetrating one that really promotes an understanding of the music.

Even the purely musical interpretation, however, is clear and vivid only when the tempos, the dynamics, and the instrumental rendition are calculated not for musical experts and Janáček specialists but for a receptive, yet unprepared audience.

Another principal factor of the interpretation is the translation of the stage works into other languages. Precisely because Janáček is and will remain a phenomenon, and because his inspiration and influence will be felt strongly in the future, it is necessary for his work to be spread to all countries. However, since all the singing in his work is governed primarily by the melody of the spoken sentence, it is imperative not only for the translation to be as faithful as possible to the words and music but also for the requirements of diction and melody of the new language to be considered to the greatest possible extent.* Unfortunately, there is proof that until now this has not been done everywhere. In the fourth place—and to no lesser extent than the other factors—the manner of vocal rendition is of decisive importance to the comprehension of the work and its intentions. Let us not forget that to the vast majority of opera singers vocal sound is more important than incisive diction, and that they strive for a vocal cantilena even where it is completely out of place. In Janáček's work the pure arioso appears only in short stretches and in scattered instances. The singing voice is used predominantly for verbal expression or for characterizing the individual and the situation. A cantabile, when it does occur, is much more often assigned to an instrumental part, where it expresses the "unspoken." I remember a performance of *Katia Kabanova* in which the singers did not sing much differently from the way they do in a Puccini opera. The work was incomprehensible and boring.

On the other hand, when I staged *The Sly Little Vixen* at La Scala in Milan I found that the singers, who are certainly more at home in the Italian bel canto than any others, were almost without exception captivated by Janáček's language and type of expression. They allowed themselves, although not without resistance and with a great expenditure of energy, to be led to the proper style. The working relationship was really a very good one, and the performance, before an audience totally unused to Janáček, an unequivocal success. I am using this example to call attention

*This last statement would make an excellent credo for the translators of all works for the musical theater. Ed.

to the principles of interpretation that seem most important to me, for I consider Janáček revolutionary, not only thirty years but even forty or fifty years after his death; his work points the way for the music theater of the present and of the future.

10

The Undistorted *Carmen*

(This article was printed in the program booklet of the Komische Oper, on the occasion of its new staging of *Carmen* on January 4, 1949. Until that time very few attempts had been made to present *Carmen* with the original spoken dialogue, which explains why the staging was viewed by many as an "experiment." In 1972, Felsenstein again staged *Carmen* at the Komische Oper, and of course again in the dialogue version. By then it had been published in a French-German edition, with Felsenstein's German translation and edited by Fritz Oeser, by the Alkor-Edition in Kassel.

It should be stated that the difference between the two versions rests not merely on the use of dialogue versus recitative; there is a considerable amount of Bizet's music in the original which presumably at the time was found to be either too difficult or too bold, and which in Guiraud's version had been either eliminated or replaced by simpler passages.

It may be of particular interest to the American reader that when the Metropolitan Opera restaged *Carmen,* also in 1972, it used the original version with the French dialogues, although they were substantially shortened. Ed.)

The restoration of the original version of *Carmen* has, as expected, stirred up some lively discussions. Surely, the work of Georges Bizet and his librettists, Meilhac and Halévy, is at the very least not inferior to the later recitative version usually presented. Of course, the most interesting judgment would be that of an audience who could listen to the original version completely without prejudice, but such people are undoubtedly in the minority. The overwhelming majority are so familiar with the customary recitative version of this extraordinarily popular work that, consciously or unconsciously, they are continually comparing what they are seeing and hearing with what they already know; they cannot possibly form an unbiased opinion.

I have been intensely occupied with *Carmen* for a long time, both as a stage director and as a translator of the text, and I am particularly surprised to find in nearly all reviews and discussions the idea, perhaps not always clearly stated, of coming to terms with a "novel interpretation," as though an experiment had been undertaken with a valid and well-known work. Exactly the opposite is true, however. Whether this version appeals to you or not, it is the one intended by the composer and therefore the authentic one, since the generally known recitative version was created only after Bizet's death.

What we are offering is not an adaptation; it is a nearly literal translation of the French original, manifestly closer to the wording of the libretto used by Bizet than any other translation until now.* Before we consider whether we prefer the original version with spoken dialogue or the version with through-composed recitatives, we must ascertain why the work was so substantially revised after Bizet's death, which occurred soon after the premiere of *Carmen.* Without question, the original version with dialogue makes much greater demands on a theater ensemble. First of all, not every opera singer possesses the skill to speak prose lines convincingly; furthermore, the action of the complete original version is much more logically carried out and requires far more depth in the psychological treatment of the characters. The failure of the Paris premiere in 1875 can unquestionably be attributed to the work's realism, which at that time was unknown on the opera stage and therefore considered shocking. Beyond that, the work could hardly have become popular because the

*The author is obviously referring to German translations only. Ed.

majority of opera theaters would have been faced with insurmountable difficulties in its performance. It can be said therefore that Ernest Guiraud,* by abbreviating the action and composing the recitatives, initially did his friend Bizet a great service. However, this great service unintentionally produced negative consequences: the opera was now within reach of any ensemble that could provide the necessary voices. This in turn resulted in a false emphasis; the work had fallen into the hands of those to whom vocal beauty meant more than the content of the score and the truth of its expression.

In hardly any other opera of that period can we find music which, down to the smallest harmonic and dynamic detail, was composed, like Bizet's *Carmen,* so to complement the action and the dramatic expression. This is not the place for a treatise about singing on the stage. But it is impossible to speak of a music theater unless this is the first rule: taking for granted beautiful sound and vocal skill, at every moment the singing must be a means of expression suiting perfectly the personality of the performer and the situation of the moment, as speech would be under different circumstances.

When we try to determine what it is about the opera that most *Carmen* enthusiasts are fondest of, we find that their enthusiasm stems from a vocal interpretation which, with the exception of very few passages, was not intended by Bizet. Lovers of bel canto might be greatly disappointed if they knew that the term "aria" occurs only once in the entire piece.** All the other numbers bear such names in the original as "chanson," "couplet," "scène," or "melodrama." But even the original rhythmic, dynamic, and expressive indications, of which the composer used

*Ernest Guiraud (1837–92) was a native of New Orleans, and during most of his life a resident of Paris; he was a successful composer of operas in his own right, and at one time taught Debussy. Besides being responsible for the recitative version of *Carmen,* he also orchestrated major portions of *The Tales of Hoffmann.* Ed.

**Micaela's aria in the third act.

an uncommonly great number, contradict the interpretations offered almost everywhere by even the most prominent singers and conductors; a reading of the score will easily bear this out. We must realize that the traditional interpretation, which has almost become law, has caused a different vocal and instrumental style to be foisted on the work; often there is an unwarranted lyricism —in any case, a bourgeois romanticizing—which Bizet, according to the general mood of the plot and the score, could not have intended. A combination of all this resulted in relinquishing the truly dramatic, the passionate, the expository, and the fatalistic in favor of a far more comfortable beauty.

This must also explain why the German translation of the recitative version, which in the course of several decades has become universally accepted, unnecessarily changed the original wording to such a great extent. The original text is unusually straightforward; the German version is alternately pretentious, saccharine, and occasionally meaningless. I shall mention only one example out of a hundred that could be cited. When in the first act Micaela hands José the letter from his mother, she sings (repeating the mother's instructions):

Et tu luis diras que sa mère
songe nuit et jour à l'absent
qu'elle regrette et qu'elle espère
qu'elle pardonne et qu'elle attend.
Tout cela, n'est-ce pas, mignonne,
de ma part, tu lui diras
et ce baiser que je te donne
de ma part tu le lui rendras.

The literal English translation of this would read:

And you will tell him that his mother
is thinking day and night about the absent one,
that she is grieving and hoping,
that she is pardoning and waiting.
All this, my dear girl, you will
tell him from me, won't you?

And the kiss which I am giving you,
You will give to him from me.

In the customary translation this was rendered in a way that distorted the feeling even more than the meaning:

Sag dem teuren Kind meiner Schmerzen,
Mutterliebe währt ew'ge Zeit.
Dass sie sein Bildnis trägt im Herzen,
was er getan, sie gern verzeiht.
Lebe wohl, sprach mit feuchtem Blicke
sie zu mir, und den heissen Kuss,
den ich auf deine Lippen drücke,
bring ihn dar als der Mutter Gruss.

Here is the literal English translation:

Tell the dear child of my sorrow
that a mother's love lasts forever,
that she carries his image in her heart
and that she forgives gladly what he has done.
Farewell, she said to me with moist eyes,
and the warm kiss which I am pressing upon
your lips, offer it as a mother's greeting.

In the new translation, this is rendered in the following fashion:

Sag ihm: seiner Mutter Gedanken
gingen Tag und Nacht nur um ihn.
Sag ihm, sie würde auf ihn warten
und hätte ihm schon längst verziehn.
Alles das, Micaela, sag ihm.
Sag's für mich, du verstehst mich schon.
Und diesen Kuss, den ich dir gebe,
diesen Kuss, gib ihn meinem Sohn.

And this would be the literal English translation:

Tell him his mother's thoughts are
with him night and day.

Tell him that she will wait for him
and has forgiven everything long ago.
All this, Micaela, tell him.
Say it for me, you understand,
and this kiss which I am giving you,
this kiss give to my son.*

Aside from numerous examples in the wording of the text, it is easy to prove that the recitative version of *Carmen,* which is traditional, popular, and clamored for by audiences, deviates considerably from Bizet's creation in characterization and dramatic conception as well as in vocal and orchestral treatment; but the main objection is that it ignores the motives which probably inspired Bizet and enabled him to compose this work. Of course, it is almost impossible now to disregard the more innocuous version, familiar to all opera lovers, which was responsible for the opera's worldwide triumph. Even so, it represents a distortion of the work and was never authorized by Bizet.

*Ed. apologizes for involving English as a third language and thus complicating the issue. Yet, obviously it would have been difficult to illustrate the author's point in any other way.

11

Preparation for Staging *Carmen*

by Stephan Stompor

(1972)

One of the most important factors in a music theater production is the smooth transition from the musical studies into the scenic rehearsals. First of all, the analyses of the work made by the stage director and the conductor must be brought into harmony. This is followed by discussion and a clear definition of the ideas arrived at together, including the suggestions of the stage designer, with all the performers and other participants in the production.

As a prelude to the musical rehearsals it is necessary to have a detailed understanding between the stage director and the conductor, as well as with the conductor's close collaborators, such as the director of musical studies, the chorus director, and all the assistant conductors and coaches. In most of Felsenstein's productions all these people, as well as the Dramaturgs and assistant stage directors, were assembled at the piano for a joint reading of the work; on those occasions dramatic and scenic problems, and also the determination of tempos and even questions of casting, were discussed and largely resolved. When the musical rehearsals began, an exact scenic and musical concept had already been formed; this concept was then, before the beginning of the scenic rehearsals, thoroughly explained to the performers by the stage director, who asked for their comments.

In the case of *Carmen* a joint concept of the work already existed between Felsenstein and the conductor Kitajenko, based on their earlier collaboration in Moscow; Kitajenko, although he had taken over the musical direction only shortly before the first performance, had been in charge of the musical preparation from the very beginning and thus had been present at all the scenic rehearsals. The result was a solidly established common viewpoint in regard to the knowledge of the work and the intentions of the staging. In addition to that, the three leads, who had done the roles in the Moscow production, were familiar with the ideas of Felsenstein and Kitajenko, and had only to adjust from Russian to German. This, however, proved to be quite difficult, particularly in the dialogue, in spite of much preliminary work in Moscow under the supervision of skilled interpreters and language teachers. (All this had taken place long before the first solo rehearsals in Berlin.)

After the roles had been studied musically, at least in rough outline, and the soloists were in possession of carefully edited dialogue scripts—which the Soviet artists had studied phonetically, and for the exact understanding of their meaning—Felsenstein held reading rehearsals with piano accompaniment, with the participants seated around a table, for two and a half weeks. During these sessions he explained the musical and dramatic structure of the work and, with the help of sketches, the dramatic execution. Then there were talks about the initial situation, the psychological development, and the motivation for singing in each individual case, and also discussions concerning tempo, phrasing, dynamics, and particular accents of the interpretation. Furthermore, corrections in the translation were made, problems were opened to discussion, and questions answered.

Although six to eight hours were spent every day in such group sessions, in addition to which musical rehearsals and diction classes took place, the discussions reached only the middle of the third act before the beginning of the theater's summer vacation.

This period was extremely fruitful for the later rehearsals. During these sessions complete understanding was established between the conductor, the members of the ensemble, and the assistant conductors. (At the Komische Oper, musical rehearsals run parallel with stage rehearsals until the night of the premiere and even afterward.)

Felsenstein, during the reading rehearsals, always concentrated on the most essential and most basic factors, but he also managed some intensive work on details. Time and again he called the attention of the performers to Bizet's expressive instructions. He was able to awaken their joy in the plastic shaping of the dialogues. The insights he communicated, often brought to light by questions or difficulties of the performers or of the other collaborators, helped every participant to grasp the nature of the work more completely. I shall attempt to convey with a few examples at least an approximate idea of the content and methods of these reading rehearsals, and of the explanations and definitions that were obtained during this stage of the work.

While rehearsing the dialogue between Zuniga and José, Felsenstein precisely outlined the initial situation: "José has no friends and is very lonely; he finds the other men in his regiment abominable and he is overly conscientious in order to prove himself. He is very quiet but also hot-tempered. Zuniga is the star among the officers, a lecher; although habitually a winner, in this play he becomes a loser." In another rehearsal Felsenstein said that it is easy to view Morales critically: he is a typical product of the officers' club. About Carmen he said that she is "not merely coquettish; she is possessed by a demon." This is the kind of elucidation with which Felsenstein led the actors to the inner essence of each character.

In the case of the singer portraying Carmen—although she had been excellent in the Moscow staging—the problem was to have her rediscover the correct inner attitude in a new language. In the first rehearsal Felsenstein asked her to do away with some of the "vocal padding," and in the second rehearsal he was equally adamant. "You are using the diction of an aria and not that of a chanson," he said to her. "These things in the Habanera must be *said,* not sung. You are still singing too much from the vocal cords, and not enough from the enjoyment deep inside that you have succeeded with your mesmerism."

The scene between Micaela and José was given particular attention, both in the analysis and in the execution, not only because it is an integral part of the exposition but also in order to remove from it any kind of operatic superficiality and sentimentality. Felsenstein saw this duet as an exciting and significant scene. The transition from the dialogue to the duet he characterized as an especially instructive example of the music theater, and he challenged the singers to find their personal expressions ("What is not your own is not valid").

Lieutenant Zuniga, in Felsenstein's staging, is much more sharply profiled than usual, and this was set up during the early rehearsals, although at first only verbally. Felsenstein called the dramaturgic composition of the scene with Zuniga, José, and Carmen, in which she answers the questions of the examining officer saucily with her "tra-la-la," close to Shakespearean. "Zuniga desires Carmen; she senses this and takes advantage of it. He weighs two possibilities (preceding her 'tra-la-la'): to pardon her or to have her jailed and then to visit her in her cell. Carmen enjoys her hold on the two men. Before she sings the 'tra-la-la' she does not know what she is going to do, but suddenly it comes to her in a flash. She thinks: 'Either he will beat me, and then I will make fun of him in front of everybody, or else I will find a way to make him pay attention to me, and then I can show him all my power.' The daring she displays is completely incomprehensible to the others." In order to make all this clear, Felsenstein says to the Zuniga, "You must not rehearse your words, but rather your intentions."

This clarification of the "subtext," the intentions underlying the spoken words, was one of the most important purposes of the reading rehearsals.

After ten days of rehearsing, dedicated to analysis and discussion of the first act, Felsenstein summed up the common objective as follows: "The dramatic exposition is tighter than I have found in any other play: Carmen's fight for her life, the rivalry between José and Zuniga, José's conflict, Zuniga's conflict. All this must be made clear."

In the further course of the action the situations were just as precisely outlined. What Felsenstein said during the analysis of the so-called Flower Song could be applied to all the reading rehearsals: "We are dealing with the *composer's* intentions." As to the piece itself, he remarked that it is not merely a narrative but a confession. He stressed the unbridgeable gap between Carmen and José by calling attention to the fact that only a small part of their quarreling is being shown on the stage.

His theme, often restated, was applicable to every single situation: "In every statement on the stage the things that you think and believe must be stronger than the things you say. For the performer there must be no pauses, only caesuras." Felsenstein feels that *Carmen* is a perfect example of a drama with music in which singing becomes necessary. Time and again he referred to "the masterly score in which everything scenic is composed. Bizet's music is action."

The reading rehearsals opened new vistas not only for the performers but also for the other participants. Felsenstein's clear formulations, always based on exact knowledge of the work and always designed to help the interpreters, became a secure, accurate basis for the subsequent scenic and musical work of the stage rehearsals.

12

Felsenstein Analyzes the Tragedy of *Carmen*

(1972)

It is impossible to interpret the entire story of *Carmen* within a short space of time; for that it is too diversified and complicated. I shall attempt, however, to deal with its most significant points: who is Carmen, who is José, who is Micaela, who is Escamillo? Where do they come from and what are the motivations for their actions?

In Mérimée's novel, Carmen is a young girl offered for sale by a one-eyed pimp who considers her his property. She is a very beautiful girl, a Gypsy, and admirably suited to her calling. She is primarily occupied with love but has not as yet experienced the great love for which every trait of her character seems to predestine her. In that way she is not unlike Violetta in *La Traviata.*

In the play by Meilhac and Halévy she is a worker in the famous —or infamous—cigarette factory in Seville, which in popular fiction is the scene of many lurid happenings. But her activity in the factory is only a camouflage for her real occupation: she is a leading member of one of Spain's biggest bands of smugglers, headed by the spectacularly gifted Dancairo. She is also the "chief whore," whose task it is to intervene in particularly difficult conflicts with the customs officers, the police, and the army, and to make the gentlemen in authority more pliable. Two other "ladies" work at the same trade—Frasquita and Mercedes, who are not Gypsies.

Often, in the customary interpretation of *Carmen,* too little importance is attached to the band of smugglers. Naturally, every member of the band must be able to prove a legitimate occupation when faced by the authorities and all occupations are represented in the group. Under the leadership of Dancairo, who is exceptionally skillful, the band manages to stay beyond the reach of the police force for many years. The headquarters of the group is the tavern of Lillas Pastia, on a run-down feudal estate with subterranean passageways, about three miles from Seville. This is an essential fact in the story.

Carmen is an erotic woman, and she delights in being the focal point of the group around her. This need, as is proved later, stems from her craving for a great amorous adventure, of which she herself is unaware. Like Violetta, she despises love as such; it is abhorrent to her to yield to a man. What intrigues her is to achieve domination. And this woman, who believes herself to be free from the insanity of love, who derides love, becomes—this is the actual content of the drama—the victim of a great and total love experience.

Before continuing with the story I must say something about the other principal characters.

José hails from Navarra and is of peasant stock. He is a strong, simple fellow but not stupid, and has been strictly raised by his mother in the Catholic faith and with a firm sense of morals. Excitable and quick-tempered, he becomes involved in a fight during a ballgame and fatally wounds a friend. Pursued by the police, he is forced to leave his home province and finds refuge in a regiment of dragoons in Seville. This sounds strange: usually a regiment of dragoons would not offer a refuge to anyone. However, it is a special company of the regiment that accepts him, a company whose task it is to guard the cigarette factory; police protection is no longer adequate, in view of the mischief being staged there by the women. It is an almost punitive assignment which I might compare—if you will permit a slight exaggeration—with the Foreign Legion. The company consists mainly of ex-convicts and men with an otherwise shady past. These fellows, including the officers, subsist primarily on filthy jokes, on the cheapest kind of amusement, which is already perverted to such a degree that they no longer even derive any pleasure from the cigarette girls. Now they are on the lookout for other diversion.

In this company José, desperate over his crime and dazed by his misfortune, stands out in sharp contrast to the others. He is unhappy and is determined to do penance for his sin. Thus he becomes a very conscientious soldier, whose only aim is to be discharged as soon as possible, in order to rejoin his mother. Naturally, since he keeps his distance from the others, they treat him with derision, making him the butt of their jokes. And so he leads a lonely and tortured existence, longing for his home and his mother.

Micaela is an orphan who, when she was perhaps six or eight years old, was adopted by José's mother. (The exact time is not specified in the play; at the time of our action she is seventeen years old.) José had grown up with her. It is important to note that José committed his crime when Micaela was about fifteen years old. This means that when he last saw her she was still his childhood playmate, his sister, his companion. He had never seen her as a woman. This explains his surprise in her when she visits him in Seville at the instigation of his mother.

Escamillo is an outstanding bullfighter; at this time he is the most famous matador in all of Spain. There is hardly a woman in Seville who does not have his portrait hanging over her bed. His earnings are very high and he uses them to make a big splash, hiring the best picadors to protect himself and underwriting enormous publicity for himself to drive up the prices of admission.

Until a short time ago I was not aware of the earning potential of a bullfighter in Spain. Then last summer one of my friends, during a vacation on the fashionable Mediterranean coast of Spain, met a well-built man, about forty years of age, whose body was covered with scars. The man owned a fantastic mansion, and had a splendid, gleaming yacht anchored nearby. As it turned out, he was a very successful bullfighter who at the age of forty —no longer young for that profession—was already a millionaire. Asked why he was still practicing the dangerous calling, he said, "I am intoxicated by applause. The acclaim of the crowd is my lifeblood. One of these days bullfighting will finish me, but I cannot give it up." This story helps to explain Escamillo's behavior, and also why he spends so much for publicity. He is a marvelous-looking man, adept at all sports.

This much in regard to the characteristics of the four leading characters. Now to the story itself.

The soldier José, initially a completely uninteresting and unknown man, is on guard duty in front of the cigarette factory. Every day many people come to the plaza to see the changing of the guard. Other spectators—townspeople and peasants, workers and loafers—come here to watch the girls come out during the work break at the factory.

For many of the working girls shredding tobacco is the only legal possibility for making a living, but it is the one that pays the least. Tobacco shredding is assigned exclusively to women, and at such low wages that the majority of them turn to prostitution on weekends in order to be able to subsist at all. Carmen, the only Gypsy among them, is hated because of her inexplicable "wealth" (in comparison with the others) and also because she is a Gypsy. Furthermore, she is more beautiful than the others, owns better clothes, and has infinitely more success with men.

The factory girls lead deplorable and tragic lives. About a hundred workers are crowded into a very small room, with the temperature reaching above 100 degrees Fahrenheit. Normally, the work breaks would be used to breathe a bit of fresh air, to drink a glass of milk, to eat a sandwich. This does not happen here. The girls are not addicted to nicotine, but they smoke the cigarettes made in their factory for reasons of publicity and at the same time they display their own charms, which are revealed freely since in such heat their working clothes consist of next to nothing. During the break every girl tries to find among the dandies on the plaza one who can be counted on for a night of the weekend. The girls have no time for relaxation. Even Carmen often uses the work break for the same purpose. Unconsciously, she needs the success here to compensate for her lack of fulfillment in love.

José is not interested in whores, but he is a man of passion nonetheless. He must have seen Carmen several times—it is impossible that he sees her today for the first time—but he has never been really aware of her before.

Carmen has planned something new for today's break, something absolutely original. After all the other girls are out on the plaza Carmen, eagerly awaited, bounces in last and sings the lilting, provocative song with which she expects to please the crowd.

José, who ordinarily despises the cigarette girls, suddenly finds himself giving her his complete attention. He is struck by her attractiveness, but he cannot admit this to himself, for obviously she is a whore, like all the others. He tries to ignore the impression she is making upon him, and maintains an aloof attitude much in contrast to the general enthusiasm over Carmen. This puzzles her; that a man should not be interested in her, obviously neither desiring her nor finding her particularly beautiful, is a new experience. What is more, she cannot tolerate it. "He will make amends to me for this, and all these people will be my witnesses," she says.

If José had not turned his back on her, or if he had stared at her like everybody else, the whole drama would not have taken place. I point out this circumstance to stress the element of coincidence which in this play is repeatedly used as a dramaturgic device. Carmen manages to arouse this young man: first he becomes interested, then feels desire, and at last he almost loses his mind over her. He is inflamed with a passion that he has never known before. The crowd honors Carmen with deafening applause. The sound of the factory bell is heard, and the work break is over.

After Carmen has satisfied her desire for revenge with sensational success and is about to disappear into the factory, she inexplicably turns around once more, approaches him in the fever of her triumph, and—consciously or unconsciously—works magic on him, part of Gypsy superstition: she throws him the acacia blossom which she had worn for her entrance, striking him with it on his forehead.

José is known to us as a naïve peasant lad by his initial conversations with Morales and Zuniga. As soon as the acacia blossom strikes him, he is spellbound, and from then on he walks through the action as if driven by an unknown power. Now the tragedy begins.

At this moment Micaela appears, a messenger from the world from which José has just become alienated. She comes from his mother, about a day's journey from Seville. After José joined the military, his mother had moved away from their native village in order to be closer to him. Now she sends Micaela, who has never been in Seville before, to find him in town. Micaela carries a letter in which the mother admonishes him to do everything he can to return home as soon as possible and also suggesting that he marry Micaela. This is a somewhat embarrassing mission for Micaela, who has been infatuated with José for some time. For a moment, José is dumbfounded by his mother's suggestion, but gradually he warms up to it as he realizes that Micaela has grown up.

I mentioned before that José is irreversibly under the spell of Carmen. When suddenly he sees Micaela he is startled: he feels trapped in his fascination for Carmen, and, Micaela at first seems to personify his mother's condemnation of his new passion. From this reaction we now recognize something completely incredible: the love of his mother and the longing for her are so strong in him that he feels her presence in Micaela. This makes him so happy that it erases the madness caused by Carmen, at least for the moment. If this is acted in a recognizable fashion, it also becomes understandable why in the following duet José sees

Carmen as an evil demon and his mother as his patron saint; it can be attributed to the almost schizophrenic situation. But we, the onlookers, must not for one moment doubt his complete submission to Carmen.

The scene ends with José's decision to obey his mother's wish and marry Micaela. At this moment horrible shrieks are heard from the factory. Women come rushing out. Clearly this is one of the reasons why the police detachment was not sufficient for the maintenance of order and had to be replaced by the military.

At this point I must introduce another character who is essential to the unfolding of the action: Lieutenant Zuniga. He is the new company commander and is in Seville for the first time. He is good-looking, quite competent, and—not unlike Escamillo—used to unfailing success with women. He can hardly wait to make the acquaintance of the cigarette factory "Sodom and Gomorrah." This leads to the conversation in which we learn of José's origin, and also the story of the murder.

Zuniga now seems inexperienced and completely helpless in the face of the outburst in the factory. In his excitement he orders José—who, in contrast to the other soldiers, would probably be fairly reliable in a difficult situation—to clear up the incident.

The quarrel of the cigarette girls over Carmen's guilt or innocence, in which Zuniga is appealed to as judge, becomes musically and textually so vehement and wild that the vocal and scenic demands are almost unrealizable.

During this development we learn the following: Manuela, one of Carmen's rivals, had boasted in front of all the girls that she was going to buy a donkey. Carmen, taking up the cudgel, had replied, "What do you want with a donkey? A broomstick would do just as well." (In the German translation the very clear formulation of the French original is somewhat softened.) The two women had lunged at each other and Manuela was left lying on the floor, cut across the face.

José walks into this situation and, flabbergasted, recognizes the accused as his beloved. He tries to cover up his confusion with rudeness and conscientiously drags Carmen before Zuniga for questioning. The interrogation ends with the arrest of Carmen who, aware of her guilt, does not even try to defend herself, but insolently attempts to make use of Zuniga's obvious desire for her. José is given the command to take Carmen to prison.

While Zuniga is writing out the order for imprisonment—which takes some time, since in his enamored state he has to start it over several times—Carmen tries with every available means to persuade José to let her escape on the way, since for Gypsies being deprived of liberty is worse than death.

Now the marvelous dialogue scene takes place, which in the usual recitative version is omitted, and which leads to the famous Seguidilla. Carmen attempts in three different ways to force José to set her free. Since she does not succeed in overcoming José's military sense of duty with charm, she tries local patriotism, claiming to come from Navarra, as he does. He believes her, but in her anxious excitement she underestimates her success and tries to reinforce her lie by further chatter. José, who has never known girls from Navarra to be chatty, becomes suspicious. Admitting that she is not "the girl from his part of the country," she reveals herself as a Gypsy. Now she stakes everything on one card: "Yes, I am a Gypsy, but you are going to set me free just the same because you love me."

It is characteristic of Carmen that even in her hopeless situation she chances beyond this self-assured statement by asking him why he had put the acacia blossom in his pocket. (As we know, she cannot possibly have seen this.) Her calculated risk succeeds; José now feels that she can see through him. He furiously throws the flower on the ground and forbids her to speak to him. "As you wish, Mister Sergeant. If I may not speak to you . . . ," she replies, and she starts to sing the Seguidilla (a perfect example of the inevitable buildup from speaking into singing). This time José loosens the rope with which she is bound.

At this moment Zuniga appears with the order for imprisonment. In accord with their arrangement, Carmen pushes José and he falls to the ground; the other soldiers trip over him and cannot prevent Carmen's escape. However, the plot was too obvious. José is arrested, demoted, and imprisoned.

The second act begins about three weeks later. Carmen has received word of what happened to José. As an expression of her deep gratitude for having set her free, she has sent him, concealed in a loaf of bread, a file to use on the prison bars and some money with which to buy civilian clothes after the escape. She now expects him night after night in the tavern of Lillas Pastia, where (in the Seguidilla) she had told him to look for her. She waits impatiently. She wants to reward him with passion such as she has never bestowed on any man but he does not appear. This to her is incomprehensible. Since she believes that he has become completely subservient to her, her only explanation is that his escape has been forcibly prevented and to her gratitude she adds her admiration for a martyr. Her impatience grows into longing, and the gratitude becomes an emotion to which she would abandon herself unreservedly for the first time. Therefore it is not surprising that when Zuniga informs her of José's release from jail her joy is so enormous that she can no longer bear it alone.

In this instant of highest excitement, again by coincidence, an unexpected encounter determines the further course of Carmen's life. A torchlight parade in honor of the famous bullfighter Escamillo passes by, and Escamillo himself, invited by Zuniga, enters the tavern. He replies to the invitation with a toast extolling the valor of the soldier, which he compares with the bullfighter's courage. The crowd greets his song of the bullfight, in its hammy overdramatization and its shameless sensationalism, with frenzied applause. Carmen is fascinated. Escamillo's imposing appearance draws her to him with erotic magnetism. His limitless conceit appears to her as an expression of male pride, of noble grandeur. The unthinkable has happened: Carmen is overwhelmed by love.

One might ask: How is this possible? Is she not completely

filled with the expectation of José? Is it not he that has aroused love in her?

This belief gives rise to the general supposition that Carmen loves José. But love is not the emotion that José has aroused in her; it is gratitude. When could she possibly have loved him? First she takes revenge on the man who wounded her pride, then she makes use of him to effect her escape, and now out of pity for the man who lost his freedom for her she wishes to reward him.

Her readiness for a great love which the waiting and impatience produced can only be brought to fruition with a tangible partner. And since Escamillo appears on the scene at this crucial time, he becomes the recipient of Carmen's feeling. Had José arrived first, that feeling would have been directed to him.

Escamillo leaves and Carmen is alone with Frasquita and Mercedes when Dancairo arrives with Remendado. The three women are reminded, to their horror, that they had forgotten the start today of the biggest smuggling enterprise as yet undertaken by the band. However, no penalty is imposed by the chief, who is usually inexorable when it comes to discipline, because, as we learn in the beginning of the famous quintet, the merchandise, worth millions, must cross two borders, and Carmen, always successful with customs officers, is absolutely indispensable. She knows, however, that her meeting with José will not take place if she carries out her duty. Despite her awareness that Dancairo will be merciless with anyone jeopardizing the enterprise—even to the point of death—she refuses, after a violent inner struggle, to participate in the Gibraltar expedition. It is almost incomprehensible that she would take such a risk; perhaps the explanation is that now, overwhelmed by love, she is even more grateful than before for the chance to have kept her freedom and has a heightened need to pay her debt of gratitude. She cannot forgo the meeting with José.

Pressed by the others, Carmen confesses the reason for her refusal. This results in a test of strength between her and Dancairo which leaves Frasquita, Mercedes, and Remendado seriously concerned about the success of the entire smuggling expedition. When immediately afterward José actually appears, Dancairo yields and, to insure Carmen's participation, offers to take her lover along.

Now the moment has arrived for which she has been waiting for three weeks. She is beside herself with joy and greets José rapturously. The new Carmen, who is now ready for a great love experience, is receiving her lover.

Again the obvious objection arises: But are the source and the fulfillment of her great love not Escamillo?

Certainly the source, but not as yet the fulfillment. This question strikes at the root of the tragedy. According to the dramatic conception of the work there is no doubt that the physical fulfillment would have taken place if the action had permitted Carmen to remain alone with Escamillo. But this is precisely what the authors did not want. Thus it becomes evident in her "confession" during the quintet that her fulfillment is bound up in her longing for the man who is about to arrive, and that this gives her the courage to face the head of the band so uncompromisingly. Naturally she acted instinctively in her exultant greeting of José: she does not know that the wonderful qualities she saw in Escamillo she now blindly transfers to José in an onrush of feeling. This is a process which often occurs in real life and it inevitably ends in tragedy.

The blissfully happy reunion is poetic in its exuberance and tenderness.

While Carmen is performing an enchanting song and dance for José the playing of retreat is heard from afar: José must return to the barracks. But how can one think of the barracks when one is in love? Now the battle starts. Carmen yields to blind fury; she curses his soldierly sense of duty. Her belief that he wishes to return to the barracks is even more devastating to him than having to leave her at this moment. With almost insane determination he faces her so violently that she stops her outburst. In greatest excitement he holds up to her the faded acacia blossom, driven by the desire to prove his love for her. He tells her that during his stay in prison, in the anguished hours of the night, the perfume of the flower conjured up a vision of her; he cursed the vision but begged God to let him see her again. This emotional piece, perhaps the most dramatic of the entire opera, is usually referred to as the Flower Song and is accordingly misunderstood and sentimentally distorted.

Carmen, struck by the depth and steadfastness of his love, uses this revelation to tie him completely to her and to her life. With a hypnotic persuasiveness she unrolls before his eyes the freedom of the Gypsy and all the splendors of the adventurous life of the smuggler, stiffling his attempts to stop her. He seems completely conquered by her when his inborn sense of duty wrests him from her embrace and forces him, despite his reluctance, to bid her a final farewell and return to the barracks.

Carmen knows that he is no longer able to do this. But even before José realizes it himself, Zuniga arrives to see Carmen, violently forcing an entry. When José disobeys the lieutenant's order to leave, Zuniga, totally drunk, slaps him. José draws his saber and undoubtedly would have killed Zuniga if it were not for the smuggelers who, called in by Carmen, immediately disarm Zuniga and take him prisoner. José, now without any hope of returning to his regiment, has no choice but to obey Carmen's wish. He is now a member of the gang, and Carmen's participation in the expedition is assured. They all depart jubilantly.

The trip to the coast, the collection of the smuggled merchandise, and the return require approximately three weeks. The happiness of the couple endures for a shorter time, for in the beginning of the third act we find Carmen rebuffing José. She is bitterly disappointed in him: he is not the idol that caused her transformation into a loving woman.

Who is this idol? Is it not Escamillo? No, it is not he; it is someone who does not actually exist. This precisely is the tragedy or, if you wish, the tragicomedy. José took the place in Carmen's life of the idolized Escamillo; it was, of course, for her a completely unconscious transference. This sounds absurd, yet it is the indisputable psychological fact without which the sequence of the action would be neither consistent nor tragic.

The disappointment and bitterness lead to a nasty interchange that drives José into retreat and Carmen into desperate, brooding loneliness. Frasquita and Mercedes are afraid that the smuggling enterprise may fail if Carmen's mood cannot be changed. They try to pull her out of her depression with the cards, reading grotesquely exaggerated prophecies in order to induce her participation. She comes over to them but her mood does not change. Carmen, inescapably caught and at odds with God and the world, now sees a betrayal even in the hallowed Gypsy art of fortune telling: fate is preordained; the cards have no power. Her denial of the Gypsy ritual leads, in the so-called Card Song, to an outburst which reveals to us the entire depth of her despair.

The smugglers also find themselves in a bad situation when Dancairo returns from his scouting expedition. He brings the news that the customs officers who had been bribed by Lillas Pastia have been relieved. To Carmen's question about the identity of the new guards he answers gloomily with the names of three extremely efficient "watchdogs." The perplexed members of the band cannot understand the joy of Carmen, Frasquita, and Mercedes, who know these three only too well. With a great burst of energy Carmen plunges into the song of the seduction of the customs officers. This initiative, born out of her despondency, pulls all the others with her and turns into a triumphal march to the customs station at the border.

Suddenly, in the deserted canyon where José has been left alone to guard the remaining merchandise, Micaela appears. Led by a mountain guide, she is in search of José. It would be appropriate to discuss here the diligence with which the girl has ascertained where to find José, and with what courage she has spurned her guide's warnings in regard to this extremely dangerous enterprise. But I have decided to limit myself to the ramifications of the tragedy of Carmen and shall therefore, in this chronological sequence, pass over the wonderful aria of Micaela, which is too seldom dramatically realized.

José, walking guard, discovers Escamillo, who, while taking a herd of bulls to Seville, has made a detour to this place in order to see Carmen. His recklessness in approaching the hideout of the smugglers can be explained only by his passion for her. The fact that José's shot misses him by a hairsbreadth he owes to José's preoccupation. José adopts a conciliatory attitude when he learns that he is facing the famous bullfighter, but this soon changes when Escamillo starts to boast about Carmen's love. A fight with knives ensues in which the blindly furious José would undoubtedly be overcome by the cold-blooded superiority of his opponent if it were not for the fact that Escamillo slips and falls.

Carmen, who at this very moment returns with the smugglers, parries the death blow without knowing the identity of the victim, and only to prevent José from becoming a murderer once again. When she recognizes the man whose life she has saved, she knows overwhelmingly that she has chosen the wrong partner in love; her distaste for José is matched by a feeling of belonging unconditionally to Escamillo.

José's desperate outburst of rage against Carmen is interrupted by Micaela, who, emerging from her hiding place, brings news of his mother's impending death. José immediately follows Micaela, but not without threatening Carmen with retribution.

Fourth act: Escamillo's bullfight has been announced with great fanfare, and the people welcome the pompous procession with lively cheers. Frasquita is there with Zuniga, Mercedes with Andres. The climax is the arrival of Escamillo with Carmen. Dressed in a bridal gown, she kisses Escamillo's sword and admits to being his wife. Frasquita and Mercedes vainly warn her against José, whom they have discovered hidden in the crowd.

Surprisingly, Carmen remains on the plaza alone, after all the others have gone into the arena. Her state betrays greatest exaltation and controlled decisiveness. She seems to seek the encounter with José, in order to break with him permanently and to begin a new life with Escamillo free from any commitment.

José, who has had warrants out against him for weeks, arrives in a completely disheveled state. He feels that he must save Carmen from what in his eyes would be the greatest disaster. He knows how much she loves Escamillo, and has seen how unreservedly she belongs to him. And yet, he not only believes in his mission but he is as convinced of its success as he is of the fiction that he is acting entirely selflessly. This faith endows him with a sinister stubbornness. It is the same superhuman strength with which Micaela in the third act was able to tear him away from Carmen.

But Carmen's happiness makes her determination insuperable. In the knowledge that she has achieved her ambition, she is invulnerable to threats from the raving man. As she tries to enter the arena to participate in the victory of her husband, she walks into the knife of José, who is not even conscious of committing murder.

When—as it happens in the majority of all interpretations—Carmen in this scene fearfully tries to flee, and José stabs her like a hunted animal, then the basic character traits of both persons, and their motivations, have not been recognized. In that case the work loses some of its human truth and significance. The real tragedy of *Carmen* is not taking place.

PART THREE

Interviews with Walter Felsenstein

13

Walter Felsenstein—Rolf Liebermann: Conversations During Rehearsals

(Rolf Liebermann, the famous Swiss-born composer of symphonic works and of several operas [*Penelope, School for Wives*] who is now general manager of the Paris Opera, was for many years the artistic director of the State Opera in Hamburg. In that capacity he invited Felsenstein in 1960 to stage *La Traviata* and again in 1962 to stage *Rigoletto.*)

"TO TAKE LITERALLY WHAT THE MUSIC SAYS" (April 7, 1962)

LIEBERMANN: Unfortunately, *Traviata* and *Rigoletto* are treated rather patronizingly, particularly in German theaters. They are allotted very little rehearsal time, usually only a few days, and sometimes we even purchase the stage sets for them from other theaters. But you have been rehearsing *Rigoletto* here for weeks with wholehearted intensity. Obviously you do not look down on it.

FELSENSTEIN: I am sure that many people do not. If it is really true that a work like *Rigoletto* is not appreciated, it is not the fault of the audiences. If this work were presented to them exactly as Verdi wrote it, they would be just as enthusiastic as they are with a sequence of unrelated vocal bravura pieces, or even more so.

LIEBERMANN: But is it not anticipation of vocal artistry that brings an audience to a Verdi opera?

FELSENSTEIN: Also the need to understand the action. You cannot look down on a Verdi opera if you are willing and able to take it seriously and to interpret it literally. Whoever finds it illogical has never examined it carefully or listened to it correctly, and has not bothered to find out what it is all about. This attitude often begins with the reading of the German translations, which in many cases are faulty.

LIEBERMANN: In Hamburg we are attempting to stimulate interest in early Verdi by using two of your techniques. First, we are revising the text in order to come closer to the Italian original; second, we are trying to play these operas exactly as Verdi composed them.

FELSENSTEIN: That is your duty. And as soon as you take a Verdi score literally, which unfortunately many interpreters are not prepared to do, it becomes a stage director's workbook. Every eighth note, every change of tempo, every dynamic indication is a scenic direction in itself. Every instrumental phrase corresponds to a scenic action or reaction. Unless the text turns everything upside down, the music alone compels you to play the drama correctly—provided, of course, that you have talented performers. I am saying this to emphasize that I reject any "conception," any personal interpretation of the piece, and also to assure you that I do not have one myself. I am simply taking literally what the music says.

LIEBERMANN: Undoubtedly, that results in true objectivity, in absolute fidelity to the work.

FELSENSTEIN: In the course of staging we must guard against a great danger. An example from one of the rehearsals: the other day I objected to the way a passage was being sung—from a musical and dramatic standpoint it seemed completely nonsensical—but I was told that this was international usage.

LIEBERMANN: Meaning bad taste.

FELSENSTEIN: Taste is a personal matter and as such has no place in an artistic interpretation.

LIEBERMANN: This brings us to the so-called operatic traditions. How do these originate and why are the audiences so attached to them?

FELSENSTEIN: Because they have been forced to accept them.

LIEBERMANN: This does not change the fact that female singers are always getting away with adding their own little embellishments to arias. Why does no one object to fermatas that are not written in the score?

FELSENSTEIN: Because the interpretation is based on bravura execution rather than on content. Verdi writes about this in his letters, criticizing his singers for being high-handed and vain. We must take Verdi literally as a composer, which means we must also accept his innovations in the field of *dramatic* composition.

LIEBERMANN: What do these innovations consist of?

FELSENSTEIN: Of keeping the traditional opera of set numbers subservient to the drama.

LIEBERMANN: But in spite of these innovations the vocal artistry has continued to attract more attention than the drama.

FELSENSTEIN: Because it is very difficult, sometimes even impossible, for us to meet the unusually strenuous emotional demands of these operas. It is only when we cannot do so that it is possible for the music to seem hackneyed.

LIEBERMANN: Strangely enough, nothing like that ever happens with *Falstaff.*

FELSENSTEIN: Because the old, experienced Verdi, having learned a number of lessons from his earlier works, decided not to risk anything that might lead to a false interpretation. The same is true in the case of *Otello.*

LIEBERMANN: However, in *Rigoletto* there are situations that are not believable because they simply are not sufficiently explained or prepared. Is it helpful in staging to consult the original literary source? Did you make use of Victor Hugo's *Le Roi s'amuse* when you did *Rigoletto?*

FELSENSTEIN: Not at all. And in the case of *La Traviata* I did not concern myself with *La Dame aux camélias* by Dumas. I think it is a mistake to use the literary source as a basis for staging an opera; it might confuse the issue.

LIEBERMANN: This means that you cannot get help from the writer who provided the literary basis, only from the librettist. What a pity that Boito did not write the libretto for *Rigoletto!*

FELSENSTEIN: Needless to say, Boito is an ideal librettist.

"EVERYTHING MUST BE SHOWN CONCRETELY"
(April 25, 1962)

LIEBERMANN: You seem to want an almost contemporary effect in your sets for this work, although it takes place during the Renaissance. I can hardly even sense a historic distance.

FELSENSTEIN: If I were to use the setting of an earlier century on the stage like a historic picture postcard, the effect would be old, distant, and dusty. But the same piece will strike you as having been dusted off when everything in the production, even the props, relates directly to the action. Through their dramatic function all things assert themselves and in this way become modern. The same is true of the costumes. A costume that is only historically accurate will always inhibit acting, since it neutralizes the personality. When, however, it is made especially to suit the actor, naturally in the basic style of the period, it will intensify his performance.

LIEBERMANN: How do you approach the visual side of the production? What, for instance, gave you the idea of playing the fourth scene underneath a bridge?

FELSENSTEIN: The scenic instructions in the vocal score are so oriented to the requirements of the nineteenth century that we were forced to invent something new. For example, according to the score, you must show a house that is cut open. That is unrealistic, and in my view disturbing, no matter how beautifully it is done. The so-called interior, from which one should not see the persons outside, must be opened realistically. And yet it must be possible for those outside to look through the cracks in the door without being seen by the people inside. This requirement stems from the famous quartet, where Rigoletto and Gilda are outside, and the duke and Maddalena inside.

LIEBERMANN: Where does the duke enter from?

FELSENSTEIN: He must be able to do it without being seen by Gilda and Rigoletto: he enters the house from above. Since the action takes place by a river, it stands to reason that his entrance could be made from a bridge. From that bridge a rock-hewn stairway leads to the ruins of a former guardhouse or customs house, which Sparafucile, who practices murder as a trade, has fixed up for his own purposes.

LIEBERMANN: In other words, your concern is to separate the necessary elements from the superfluous.

FELSENSTEIN: Precisely. I need a solitary spot, so that Sparafucile can carry on his business as hired assassin inconspicuously and can dump his victims into the river. Besides, he can hide his criminal activities behind the honorable trade of a fisherman.

LIEBERMANN: So this is why you have the fishing nets on the stage. At first glance they seem to be merely decorative, irrelevant to the action, but actually they are there for a legitimate dramatic reason.

FELSENSTEIN: And that is probably why the staging strikes you as contemporary.

LIEBERMANN: Because a drama of this kind could also play in our time.

FELSENSTEIN: A major portion of the piece is built on criminal activity. The crime must be believable *now,* looking back to the sixteenth century. Giving Sparafucile the accouterments of a fisherman is part of making the situation believable. I also find it wrong to romanticize the fourth scene. Everything must be shown concretely. The thunderstorm must appear not as a romantic but as a symbolic parallel.

LIEBERMANN: How do you work with the stage designer? What is your procedure?

FELSENSTEIN: We attempt to start on the same level from the very beginning, pushing away all preconceptions. We try to read the play as if it were completely unknown. What emerges first from the reading of an act, which is repeated several times, is not a visual impression but a series of dramatic accents. We ask ourselves how the "subtext"* of the action and the music can be made credible and visible. From this principle arises the basic structure of the action, which begins to allow some spatial relationships to take shape.

LIEBERMANN: Then the space is determined by certain actions.

FELSENSTEIN: Not only the space but the entire production, in which incidentally lighting plays a dominant role.

"HUMAN BEINGS CANNOT BE MADE ABSTRACT" (May 4, 1962)

LIEBERMANN: This morning in rehearsal you said that a performer must "create the singing." Do you mean that music must not seem to be memorized, but must in effect be discovered in the emotional situation?

FELSENSTEIN: Exactly. Unfortunately, singers are trained by their teachers to do nothing but sing. Even talented singers have lost their basic respect for music; it has become something that is simply there. But I maintain that the theater has always been a creative form of art, and the music or the words must in every case be created out of the situation. In opera one must always ask the question: could I simply say this or must I *sing* it?

*This term, coined by Stanislavski, usually refers to the unspoken thoughts of the performer while delivering a speech or singing an aria—thoughts that are necessary to complete the psychological picture in his own mind, and to add credibility to his characterization. Felsenstein apparently uses the term here in a broader, more general sense. Ed.

LIEBERMANN: You mean to say that music is justified once speech is no longer sufficient.

FELSENSTEIN: Because there is an abnormal, heightened need to communicate.

LIEBERMANN: In other words, the emotional scale demanded from an operatic performer is intensified by the music and goes beyond what is called for in a play.

FELSENSTEIN: It goes into the unspeakable, the sphere of fantasy, which can no longer be expressed through words. I consider music the strongest possible statement in the theater. However, we must understand that it is exclusively a human statement. Naturally, we can get some pleasure from actors who are like puppets, like singing marionettes, almost like musical instruments. But I feel that there must be *singing human beings* on the opera stage.

LIEBERMANN: Here we come to the famous alternative: whether to present opera in a extremely stylized manner or to allow the performance to develop through the intensifying of human emotions.

FELSENSTEIN: Occasionally the two may touch each other. Stylization as an end in itself is antitheatrical, but a production can come into its own even when it is stylized as long as the stylization remains subordinate. On the other hand, a highly stylized production which verges on being abstract cannot, in my opinion, be intelligible to an audience.

LIEBERMANN: It seems to me that a pure abstraction cannot fulfill the purpose. Since there are real human beings on the stage, there will certainly be the generation of real emotions.

FELSENSTEIN: If one wishes to be abstract it is best not to use human beings for it. A human being is a reality. If I try to use this reality abstractly, I am simply guilty of wrongly utilizing my basic material.*

*Ed. wishes to call special attention to this closing statement, which in three concise sentences establishes the basic principle that separates Felsenstein from many other contemporary directors of the musical stage.

14

Walter Felsenstein—André Boll: A Contribution to the Discussion of the Music Theater

In 1951 the periodical *Le Théâtre dans le Monde,* published by the International Theater Institute in Brussels, commissioned the well-known French critic André Boll to direct an inquiry to the leading European stage directors concerning the possibilities of revitalizing the musical theater.

Here is André Boll's preface to the inquiry:

> I am convinced that a reform of staging would attract a broad public to the various forms of musical theater. By reform I do not mean simply a visual reshaping (sets, costumes, lighting) but also a style to be newly created for each work and for the stage actions of its performers.
>
> Today theatergoers on the whole lack the patience for the traditional and often ridiculous usages associated with opera. Justifiably, they refuse to admire singers who stand next to the prompter's box to deliver their big arias, or to accept the stereotyped gestures of the chorus and supernumeraries as sincere. They cannot be excited by pot-bellied lovers and obese heroines. And their attitude has a solid basis. They want to believe the story that is being told to them. Moreover, they demand that the action be plausible, and even the most beautiful chords, the most subtle harmonies, and the most seductive melodies can no longer blind the public to the unlikely aspects of the plot. Opera contains theater, and this rule appears to have been largely forgotten.

The time has come for the world's great treasures of music to shake off the antiquated frames in which they have been placed and to become part of a living art again. The question arises now whether the musical theater, in order to continue its existence, can be satisfied with the cultivation of the traditional forms, such as grand opera, opera buffa, lyric drama, or operetta, or if perhaps the creative power of the musicians of our time will bring forth some new forms.

We agree with Jacques Copeau* that we must again inject genuine dramatic life into the musical theater. It is not our intention to resurrect here the perennial quarrels between the great reformers, such as Gluck, who subordinated the music to the action, or Mozart, who elevated the music above the action, or perhaps Wagner, who desired, without being able to put it into practice, a "total" art. However, in our opinion we must question whether many of the most important composers early in this century did not perhaps intentionally neglect the stage aspect of their creations in order to serve the laws of musical composition.

BOLL'S QUESTIONS AND FELSENSTEIN'S ANSWERS

BOLL: The working domain of the opera stage director—or the director of any other type of musical theater—is far more comprehensive than that of a drama director. Does this not make it more difficult to achieve unity and originality in the staging of opera?

FELSENSTEIN: In this era of the ascendancy of the stage director we unfortunately attach more importance to a director's interpretation of a work than to the desire to have the work itself perfectly realized. We must reject any interpretation whose primary aim is to produce an interesting performance but which does not carefully explore the intentions of the composer and the author and

*Jacques Copeau (1879–1949), French theatrical producer, and at one time head of the Comédie française, who pioneered for the simplification of theatrical productions. Ed.

try to fulfill them as closely as possible. Anyone who thinks he can reshape or modernize a valuable work would do better to have a new work written for him, rather than to misuse the existing one for his own purposes.

A stage director must have a forceful personality, first of all to be able to convey unmistakably the original substance of a work by the means that are most likely to reach his audience. Beyond that, he must be able, by his own methods, to help appropriately cast singers, and also the conductor and designer, become profoundly familiar with the work, and to induce them to bring forth a highly personal interpretation, but one that is completely faithful to the work, according to the laws of the theater.* In no case may the stage director confine himself to spatial and choreographic arrangements, and in no case is he allowed to use the singers as animated marionettes. Nor may he arrive at the staging without the conductor's collaboration. He must see to it that the creative reshaping of a work by the singers in conjunction with the conductor is done according to the demands of the score, and will not be disturbed by inventive afterthoughts of the conductor. So much for unity and originality in the staging of opera.

BOLL: Should the staging of a musical work be based more on the score than on the libretto? What should be done in a case where libretto and score are not completely fused into one another?

FELSENSTEIN: Opera staging should primarily be based on the score, since every good score contains all the scenic instructions for the one who knows how to read it. In all works of high quality the libretto and score harmonize with each other, as they did

*This sentence conveys perfectly the impression of a spectator at one of Felsenstein's productions: everything seems in place, as far as the work itself is concerned, and yet it is highly personal and unlike any other interpretation of the same work. Ed.

from the moment they came into being, and not one of these works contains purely symphonic portions. Every one of them was composed for the stage, and for the stage alone; however, they all need to be interpreted by performers who know as much about music as they do about the kind of singing which is more than the functioning of the larynx.

BOLL: During the musical preparation of a work, which is the appropriate moment, in your opinion, for the stage director to take over?

FELSENSTEIN: The musical preparation of a work cannot even begin until the music director, the assistant conductor, and the stage director have agreed on all facets of the work. And it is irrelevant whether we are speaking of a new work or of one from the classical repertory. A stage director who has nothing to contribute to the preparation of the vocal passages and to the expressive shaping of the portions of the score that are not sung should not be staging a work of the musical theater.*

BOLL: Do you think that it is still possible to "dust off" great masterworks of the repertory and bring them into the spirit of our time?

FELSENSTEIN: The great masterworks of the repertory are almost all timeless, in respect to both the score and the libretto. In my opinion they do not need to be "dusted off." This is the kind of offense that has been committed for decades, mostly out of negligence or lack of knowledge. Looking at the international scene, we can easily see that only the smallest percentage of the

*This perhaps somewhat puzzling passage undoubtedly is a reference to Felsenstein's conviction that while a singer is on the stage, all the music played by the orchestra belongs to him, and must seemingly be created by him; therefore he must master the orchestral phrases as completely as the ones that he sings. Ed.

so-called experts really knows and understands the original form and meaning of these works. A carefully thought-out staging, planned down to the smallest emotional reaction of every singer, would be the equivalent of a new discovery of any of these works.

BOLL: In the case of works with spoken dialogue—for instance, *Carmen*—should the words be spoken as they would be in a play or in some other way?

FELSENSTEIN: Interpolated prose as powerful as that in Bizet's *Carmen* must be studied with the basic melodic quality of the work in mind. These texts require an entirely realistic interpretation, but must never degenerate into private conversation. *Carmen* is a perfect example of the alienation from the theater which the international opera stage has experienced. Bizet composed the music for the libretto by Meilhac and Halévy. He certainly had a reason for breaking into the music with dialogue. However, every measure of his music expresses a profound relevance to the entire action. The reality and directness of his approach were so revolutionary that they shocked the audience at the world premiere. It is probable that without the good offices of Ernest Guiraud (who replaced the dialogue by recitative) the opera would never have started its triumphal procession over the stages of the world, but this arrangement, although responsible for popularizing the work, is nevertheless a distortion and falsification of Bizet's score. Yet, only highly accomplished singing actors were ever able to perform the sung and spoken portions with equal mastery.

Worst of all, the recitative version caused the work to be handed over to the "opera industry," which took incredible liberties with the interpretation. For various reasons—to please the public or to feed personal, instrumental, or vocal vanity—adulterations crept in which, in conjunction with translations into other languages that distorted the meaning, led to interpretations totally foreign to the spirit of the author. From the point of view of genuine theater, the work could no longer be taken seriously.

BOLL: Do you believe that with due respect to the music the focal center should always be the dramatic action?

FELSENSTEIN: There is only one focal center, the one created by the music. Every stage movement that does not follow the score meticulously is wrong. No opera in the classical repertory is an exception to this rule. Only the so-called musical experts who do not relate to the theater have managed over the years to give an abstract, isolated significance to operatic music, and they were encouraged in these tendencies by theatrical ineptitude and by lack of musicianship on the stage. The dichotomy of "music" and "stage" has been produced artificially; it does not emerge naturally from any of the great masterworks.

15

Walter Felsenstein—Horst Seeger: Opera in Films and on Television

(First published in a book, *Film-Kaleidoskop,* by Henschel-Verlag, 1971. Horst Seeger, now the Director of Opera at the Dresden State Theaters, was for many years the head of the dramaturgy department at the Komische Oper.)

SEEGER: Operas specifically written for television, for which we foresaw a great future when television first became popular, have not made great strides after all. On the other hand, operas from the classical repertory have been televised a great deal. How do you account for that?

FELSENSTEIN: I do not believe it has anything to do with the type of work. There can be good operas, planned for the television screen and its potentialities—I am sure they exist—and there can also be bad ones. This is no different from the stage. What is decisive is whether a constructive relationship exists between the creators of an operatic work (I mean specifically the librettist and the composer) and the group that produces it. The artistic fate of an opera on television, if it is basically of good quality, depends primarily on the type of contact made between the interpreting artists and the technicians. This is out of the hands of the composer. He can furnish the basic materials, but he is in no position to influence the progress of the production or the final result. Perhaps this is the reason for the lack of success of some of the television operas that you mentioned.

SEEGER: Do you believe that it makes more sense to take an opera production which has been successful on the stage and change it to fit the particular needs of television, or would you, if you had the time, give preference to a television studio production of an opera from the classical repertory?

FELSENSTEIN: The television studio productions, such as I used for my presentations of *The Sly Little Vixen, Otello,* and *The Tales of Hoffmann,* are naturally the best way at this time for me to reach a larger segment of the public. I had previously staged those three operas at the Komische Oper, and they were in the repertory for a long time. Still, this could not induce me simply to have the stage productions projected on the television screen—for documentation, as it were. That would be a task for theater historians.

However, I did try to document—if I may stick to this wording—the conceptions on which the stage productions had been based, and which unquestionably had contributed to their success. The documentation of a stage conception, which must be undertaken with the greatest variety of filming devices and camera techniques—modern as well as traditional—is a job whose difficulty increases with the amount of detail. Yet, we know from experience that it is possible to adapt an opera production to film needs without doing violence to the basic rules of artistry and the original working method.

SEEGER: Film and television lack the immediacy of partnership with the audience, the lifeblood of a theatrical performance. Does this make a great difference to your adaptation?

FELSENSTEIN: I must admit that I prefer the cinema to television as a medium. We prepared the scripts meticulously for our recent opera films and naturally we employed all the film devices that could help clarify our original intentions, including the degree and tint of color. When it comes to television reception in the homes, this factor, for example, is unfortunately out of our control; by one millimeter of improper focusing the spectator may destroy a brightness, a tint, or even a color, no matter how carefully it has been worked out, or he may even change its artistic meaning into the very opposite. I do not believe I can operate with such a wide, and for the moment unavoidable, margin and that is the reason I prefer the cinema, as I said before. Naturally, I had in mind a larger group of spectators than the one usually gathered around a television set; and I envisioned a theatrical experience roughly resembling the kind found in live theater, even though a genuine, "participating" reaction could not occur.

SEEGER: You formerly produced cinema films and in recent years you have created a few opera films for German television. Are the differences in the artistic methods so fundamental that it is possible to talk about them specifically? As a rule, we mention only a few basic conditions of the television film which have to do with the enclosed, intimate sphere of reception and the size of the picture. Television plays and films are tailored to these conditions. But the continuity and dramatic structure of an opera from the stage repertory are inalterable. Have you discovered an in-between method? And do you look upon it as a real answer to the problems of televised opera?

FELSENSTEIN: I do not believe that film and the opera stage differ fundamentally from each other in respect to dramatic structure and continuity. Film has its own techniques for emphasis, such as cutting, montage, and so on, and music provides opera with equivalent possibilities, so that in both forms of art we have a great deal of leeway. The inappropriate use of film devices can change and even distort the original concept of an opera production. On the other hand, these devices make possible certain accents in the film for which there is no opportunity on the stage because of technical limitations but which the interpreter would like to stress. Thus film can sometimes afford us greater clarity.

SEEGER: How did you come to terms with acoustical problems?

FELSENSTEIN: That is a very special question. Verdi, Offenbach, and Janáček, since they were not film composers, based their dynamic instructions on their knowledge of acoustics within the space of a theater. This is not limited to dynamics only: even melody-shaping, phrasing, and orchestration in good scores are calculated with the space in mind, allowing for a certain distance between performer and audience. Therefore in an opera score there are no acoustical "close-ups," as it were. But in film we cannot possibly forgo the short distance, the close-up, or the result would be nothing more than photographed theater.

I have tried to cope with this difficulty by instructing my performers to substitute for acoustical dynamics the dynamics of intensity—in other words, to substitute expressiveness for volume. This has mostly worked very well; and in this fashion we have avoided the impression of a continuous changing of distance—something that could happen very easily if in making the film every "close-up" were to correspond to a "forte" and vice versa.*

*Other opera film producers have handled this problem differently: they had the video and audio portions recorded at different times. This, of course, is very easy for the singer who can separate the problems of singing and acting, but it also looks easy to the spectator and thus loses credibility; action and sound no longer seem to blend.

Having seen three of Felsenstein's opera films myself, I can bear witness to the fact that his method does work very well. The passionate expression is there when it is needed, and yet one never gains the impression of a singer screaming high notes at the camera. Ed.

16

Walter Felsenstein—Vilem Pospisil: The ABC of Stage Direction

Vilem Pospisil is a well-known Czech writer on musical subjects, and the director of the music festival "Prague Spring." This interview appeared in the Prague periodical *Hudebni Rozhledy* in October, 1962.)

While I was watching some scenes directed by Professor Felsenstein, a few questions occurred to me that I asked him during intermissions.

Perhaps the most striking element of all Felsenstein stagings is their rhythm, their increased expression, their overflow—or so it seems at first—of gesture and movement. There are movements of all kinds, all dimensions, and they are quite deliberately planned. The stagings grow out of an admirable mixture of poetic imagination and a sense of reality which sometimes appears brutal and almost bordering on naturalism. Hence my first question:

In your opinion how do stylization, realism, and naturalism relate to each in the music theater?

FELSENSTEIN: Stylization in opera is necessary. My production of Britten's *Midsummer Night's Dream* was stylized, but realistically so. The stylization of experimental productions starts with the visual, the decor, not with the actor. Although the stage sets of my *Midsummer Night's Dream* are strongly stylized, however, there is no doubt that they represent a forest. Naturally, the actors reinforce the realism of the forest by the manner in which they act. Naturalism obviously is not allowable on the stage. It is without poetry. Every stage happening, together with the music, must derive from poetry. The stage must be a poetic effusion, a poetic expression, an image, an allegory; for if reality is reproduced photographically, it obviously loses every poetic quality. The actor must project himself into a character other than his own, and he must express the feelings of that character. The expression of his own feelings would be naturalism.

All unnatural movements should be avoided on the stage as much as any kind of "just being there," like the so-called supernumerary. But ornamental stylization is prohibited, since it turns human beings into puppets and they lose their credibility.

You said that in contemporary experimental stagings the stylization begins with the set. Can this kind of stylization reach the point of being abstract?

FELSENSTEIN: Anything abstract is inadmissible on the stage. Of course, there are certain intermediate stages. I am in complete agreement with economy in staging. But the spectator must always know where something plays and by whom it is played. Today's avant-garde does not take sufficient cognizance of that. Stage directors and set designers must not be tempted to move out of the audience's reach for the sake of "originality." I may have an excellent idea, but if I cannot convey it to the actor so that he will communicate it convincingly to the audience, it is worthless. There are stage directors who are blessed with an abundance of excellent ideas but cannot express them. Then there are directors who may only have five ideas but know how to make them effective; these are more valuable.

What can you say about illusion on the stage?

FELSENSTEIN: The illusion on the stage must be perfect, without any gaps, no matter what produces it—language, voice, lighting, or stage set. However, illusion is not what is being produced but what the spectator sees, what his impression is. For that reason a barren stylization cannot be permitted. It is foreign and hostile to the theater, and also to imagination and poetry.

Our conversation focused subsequently on a question that had come to my mind while I was reminiscing on Felsenstein's production of The Bartered Bride. *Without mentioning that opera I asked what was meant by a staging "faithful to the work."*

FELSENSTEIN: By that I mean executing the work according to the intentions of the composer—looking for the meaning of the work, not for the right notes or the right words. I can be faithful to the work even when I make cuts. Of course, everything starts with the fact that I must know the music. But it is not sufficient merely to know the notes or the text. Both are only auxiliary devices which the composer and the librettist use to express themselves. The words of Goethe's *Faust* are not a play, nor are the notes of *The Sly Little Vixen* an opera in themselves. In the course of my forty years in the theater I have learned that it is not always easy to get acquainted with a work. When I ask someone whether he knows *The Marriage of Figaro,* he will answer in most cases, Of course, I know every note of it. Sometimes he may not even know the plot, but the plot, after all, is not essential to the true meaning of the work. It is rather an auxiliary device that allows the author to express himself. To know the work therefore means to understand the intentions of the author, and to see them clearly enough to be able to communicate them to the audience.

Literal "faithful" execution does not mean anything. In Smetana's *Bartered Bride* I made two changes. I moved the Mařenka-Vashek duet to the first act and I repeated the scene of the comedians. These were decidedly infringements, but they tightened the dramatic action. The duet is very important for the exposition. Done in the tavern (second act), it impairs the continuous flow of the drama. The tavern must be cleared of people in order to make the duet possible. There was one disadvantage to my solution: the second act became much shorter. But being able to present the conflict between Jenik and Kecal without interruption was a decided improvement. These infringements were not "faithful to the work," but they are defensible because they deepen the content and the meaning, make them more accessible. Otherwise, I did not alter anything. I can understand the objections of my Czech colleagues to placing the duet in a different spot, but I cannot understand why they have not protested the German translation by Max Kalbeck, which grossly distorts the meaning of *The Bartered Bride.* I was the first to provide a complete and faithful translation of the text to which Smetana composed his music.

One more word on the subject of being "faithful to the work." Today's avant-gardists often have good ideas, as I have said before. They try to create something new, and for that reason they should be supported. But too often they are so overwhelmed by their own ideas that they are not interested in aspects of the work that do not implement these. Hence we often find productions in which there is no more than one idea, usually pictorial, complemented in a way that leaves the meaning of the work entirely untouched. But when the stage director cares for nothing except originality—nothing except leaving the accustomed, traditional channels behind—with no concern about whether the audience understands him or not, he is so arrogant that he ought to be restrained from directing.

The most essential question has not yet been asked. The characters appearing in the operas are, of course, not singers; they are human beings who in unusual situations can only express themselves through singing. And singing which is not justified emotionally has no business on the stage. Certainly it cannot exist in the theater without a certain kind of passion. The main point is that in lieu of false, rhetorical passion we must offer what I should like to call "passion of the soul." The audience must never recognize singing as the practicing of a professional skill. Every kind of reality is worthless if the naïve spectator is not forced to believe that the singer *must* sing. No one should ask: "Why does this person not speak instead? It would be easier to understand him." Singing is exalted expression, concentration on its highest level. Such concentration, however, can emerge only from a concrete situation that allows nothing other than singing at this moment, and exactly as the composer has captured it in his musical symbols. The scene of the thunderstorm in *Otello,* as you saw it, could never be spoken; it must be sung. In the theater we must create a situation that contains something new, something fresh, something elemental which cannot be repeated. Modern man has lost his connection with his creative core. But a certain longing for this creative core has remained with him. It can find its fulfillment in art.

17

Walter Felsenstein—Hans-Rainer John: A Conversation on the Tasks of the Music Theater

(Hans-Rainer John is editor-in-chief of the periodical *Theater der Zeit,* which published this interview in issue 8 of 1962.)

JOHN: Today the musical theater relies much more on traditional repertory than the legitimate theater does. For that reason our obligation to select older works and interpret them from a contemporary point of view—to uncover their ideas to the public —has grown even more pressing.

FELSENSTEIN: Aren't those works of the past significant particularly because they contain the possibility of a solid bridge to the present? Their heroes not only experience the great fundamental human emotions, such as love, sadness, hate, envy, joy, and jealousy, but they come to grips with those emotions and mature by experiencing them, thereby reaching a new level of human growth. By putting dramas of this kind of development into their specific historical setting we can reclaim them for the present as genuine "contemporary plays."

JOHN: Then why, in spite of all this, do we see so many old-fashioned performances that do not involve us emotionally?

FELSENSTEIN: The timeliness we have been talking about is not always perceptible at first glance. More often than not it reveals itself only to those who know how to penetrate into the very essence of an operatic work. Not everyone has the talent to get thoroughly acquainted with each work; I am speaking of more than just text and music. The ideas of interpretation derived from knowledge of the work must lead to a concept of staging that does the work justice. Today you hear a great deal about these concepts, but as long as they are devised for their own sake, or only to mirror the subjective relationship of the director to the work, and not to carry out the work's intentions, they are unusable. (For that reason I am firmly opposed to updating a text, revising it to make a work more timely; where this seems absolutely necessary, the freshness of the work is probably questionable to begin with, and it would be better to write a new one.) Also, the concept must be completely taken over by all who participate in the production. I believe that the quality of a stage director is measurable by the extent to which he can make his ideas of interpretation the concern of the entire ensemble. It is a long road.

JOHN: We must also remember that sometimes traditions and clichés of performance obscure the true meaning of the work.

FELSENSTEIN: There seems to have been an unwritten law that operas whose dramatic message would interfere with complacent enjoyment of the music—works that attacked and disquieted the audience with their truth—had to be smoothed down and made more pleasurable by revisions and interpretations.

JOHN: Probably a typical example of that is *Carmen.* It is common knowledge that the opera was rejected at its premiere performance because the heroine, as stated in a review written in 1875, was "a shameless woman" from whom "virtuous mothers and respectable fathers" must be protected. Thanks to the pressure from preachers of middle-class morality, this work of genius was distorted, its bold truth was weakened, and its heroine powdered and beautified.

FELSENSTEIN: The merciless tragedy of love between a peasant lad gone astray and a trollop still unfamiliar with great love does not come across in the recitative version, which is internationally used and well known. This version was written after Bizet's death by his friend Ernest Guiraud, who omitted all the spoken dialogue and composed recitatives to put in its place. Why? Because the original version failed at the premiere. Its directness and aggressiveness obviously shocked the good citizens, and there was another fairly basic reason: the majority of opera singers would have been neither able nor willing to speak the difficult prose lines properly.* It is true that Guiraud, by through-composing the opera and shortening the action, made the work popular; at the same time he simplified it, making possible an interpretation which prevails in our time but which was never intended by Bizet.

JOHN: Conventions and clichés are still remarkably influential even now. You have experienced that yourself. How often, when you had merely done away with an arbitrary interpretation, were you accused of having presented an "interesting concept by Felsenstein"? It is more comfortable to accept what is customary as right, and what is right as a personal interpretation. Perhaps we can now turn to the question of discovering a play's basic content. Let us take *Otello* for an example. What was your goal in staging that?

FELSENSTEIN: To acquaint the public with Verdi's dramatic intentions, which rarely happens with this particular opera. Even though it is based on Shakespeare's drama there are many changes. Boito and Verdi, working here, as in *Falstaff,* in ideal

*For further details on this see *The Undistorted Carmen* on page 83. Ed.

harmony, have created a totally different initial situation, and even in the profiling of the characters and in the psychology of the action they digress frequently from Shakespeare's ideas. Verdi's music contains all instructions for staging. If one tried to transpose it into words, the result would be a volume many times the size of the work itself.

It is, for instance, essential to determine Otello's life and professional career prior to the beginning of the action. Three relationships determine the course of action and the conflict: the one between Otello and Desdemona, the one between Otello and Iago, and the one between Otello and Cassio. In order to make these relationships understandable, it is necessary to trace their development from their beginnings until the start of the action, and to draw from this the conclusions we need for the interpretation. This is not the place for a dramatic analysis, but using this working method quickly reveals that it is not possible either to dismiss *Otello* as a drama of jealousy or to depict Iago as an archetypal villain.

In order to judge Otello's professional and social situation, one event, not shown on the stage but only mentioned, is very significant. The Venetian galley which carries the delegate of the doge, and thus the order to dismiss Otello, arrives twenty-four hours after the end of the victorious battle against the Turks. Since the length of time required for the trip from Venice to Cyprus under any circumstances is much more, it is evident that the dismissal of Otello in case of his victory had been decided much earlier.* Why? It can be assumed that when Otello's talent for leadership was discovered by the Venetian army, he was the head of an African resistance group against the Turks. He rose rapidly because of his outstanding ability, which within a few short years resulted in his being made commander-in-chief of the

*The formulation "in case of his victory" seems rather strange at first. What would have happened in case of his defeat? My own explanation is that in such a case his dismissal would have been unnecessary, since presumably he would not have returned alive. Ed.

Venetian fleet—in view of his race, most unusual. He had fought against the Turks on the side of Venice. Who could guarantee to the Venetian Senate that the commander, whose power over the armed forces would be unlimited after his total victory, might not suddenly hit upon the idea now of liberating his homeland from Venetian colonial rule? Therefore it would be best to recall him to a position in Venice. So as not to awaken suspicion in the army, however, his favorite, Cassio, will be made his successor. This situation does not occupy a prominent place in the totality of the action. I mention it to demonstrate the flawless conception of the work, something that could be shown equally well in any other scene.

The spectator, even in the musical theater, should participate intensely in the action; it should be an experience that enriches his perceptions. We can take it for granted that in this activation, the inclusion of the spectator, all theatrical devices will be utilized in order to make the action completely intelligible, including events not written into the text or the music. (The effort to make the text intelligible is not nearly enough.) The theater draws its breath of life from the uninterrupted dramatic tension between auditorium and stage. Once this tension is broken it is very difficult to restore. When people applaud at the end of arias, is this not a proof of boredom interrupted by a special occurrence?

JOHN: Obviously, then, every opera or operetta production must respect the laws of stage realism, the laws of scenic action. Part of it is that the singer may no longer only sing a role—in other words, bolstered by costume and makeup, he may no longer simply produce tones and present the essential points of scenario as dictated by convention. Rather, he must create a truthful and unmistakable stage personality. He must act as the character created by the librettist and the composer would act under the given circumstances, even though some experts say that having to concentrate simultaneously on singing and acting overtaxes the singer.

FELSENSTEIN: The highest aspiration within the music theater must be *not* to consider singing and acting separate functions. The difficulties to which those experts are referring are based on the false idea that there is some acting to be done onstage, in addition to which you have to sing. But singing onstage is nothing other than acting. If the physical action impedes the singing, then this action is faulty in its primary intention and in its expression. For even singing is merely a part of making music; it is no different from an instrumental part in the orchestra, which belongs to the actor no less than the singing. After all, singing is not first and foremost the technical production of vocal sounds. It is chiefly a human statement that has been evoked by an inner process and is thus insuppressible and cannot be dispensed with; it goes far beyond speaking, because it gives expression to what can no longer be conveyed by words alone. It is therefore important for the music theater to create situations that call forth music. As far as singing is concerned, it must of course be technically controlled, but we must not characterize as excessive the basic requirements of the music theater simply because certain people do not have an adequate vocal technique.

JOHN: Chaliapin once said that technique, the mastery of bel canto singing, was not all that a real singer needed, that the art of singing also included the ability to differentiate the intonation endlessly and to give different colors to the tone. This was not a physical matter, a technical accomplishment, but something to achieve by psychological means. Correctly interpreting a situation in a role, and acting accordingly, alters the inner experience. This effects change in the way the vocal apparatus functions, and it colors the voice: singing becomes more expressive. It becomes truthful and imbued with drama, and in lieu of chiché-ridden general acting there will be the portrayals of definite human beings in specific situations.

FELSENSTEIN: This is, of course, very uncomfortable for the singer. He must not only get rid of personal inhibitions and vanities (for instance, the provocation of applause); he must also study and make fruitful use of the world and preliminary history of the character he is playing. He must consistently be conscious of these, for they motivate his behavior during the episode of life being presented on the stage. The performer who portrays Rigoletto, for example, must carry within himself an exact image of Rigoletto's deceased wife. For it was she, by accepting the cripple as a husband, who provided him with the deep experience that determines his actions in the fight for his daughter's honor.

But even in the realm of music there are greater demands. A singer who knows only his vocal part, and not the entire instrumental substance, is bound to be a slave to the conductor's beat. Therefore his knowledge of the score should be so all-encompassing that he can bring forth the music himself—that he does not *obey* the music but *releases* it, so that the orchestra can accompany him exactly as the score demands.

PART FOUR

Views, Reviews, and Reactions

18

On the Reality of the Singing Human Being

by Joachim Herz

(An article on the occasion of the festive opening of the new opera house in Leipzig, 1960. Joachim Herz, a leading Felsenstein disciple, is the general manager and leading stage director of that opera house.)

Our festival week of performances to celebrate the inauguration of our new opera house can be viewed only as a steppingstone to further efforts, not as a positive achievement in itself. It is a beginning.

Not only is the theater new but also the road that we are traveling, the attempt to apply the principles of the music theater to a large repertory theater.

We who are just starting up this road have every reason to keep our goals clearly in mind. And one of these goals raises the important question of whether singing, the artistic device peculiar to opera, by its very nature removes all action from the realm of reality, or if perhaps it can become a credible and even necessary device for the representation of real actions.

It has been said that a real person who expresses his emotions and decisions in song is a paradox. Consequently, people on the opera stage should not be real people, but archetypes removed from reality, symbols, or mediums for ideas. These singing symbols often behave remarkably like traditional opera singers of an older vintage. And when these mediums for ideas must perform real actions that cannot be bypassed—cutting into their veins for the purpose of vowing blood brotherhood *(Götterdämmerung)*, stabbing someone to death, or recognizing somebody who is lying flat on his face—the hilarity caused by such breakthroughs into unconquered reality is remarkably like the amusement that unsophisticated audiences have always found in opera.

However, this may also be the fault of the creators. If they have not succeeded in making the singing appear believable and necessary, if it is possible to imagine the whole thing just as well as a spoken play, then the work itself contains the inconsistency of which we have just spoken and the endeavor to awaken it credibly to life as a musical work is a priori doomed to failure. Unfortunately, this fault can be found in many works written in our own time.

Every art brings us to recognition of a higher reality. By limiting itself in its own forms it can present its own aspect of reality more forcefully. In this way it gives us deeper insights into the conditions and potentialities of our existence.

Of all the arts the theater mirrors life most faithfully. What an audacity to add music to this excellent likeness! In truth, however, opera does not add anything to the theater; opera is not theater plus music but a completely new method of perceiving human actions visually and aurally. Opera turns into sound what lies below and beyond the external processes of life: the impulses of the will, the sentiments, the emotions. Naturally, the spoken play too makes visible in its own way what lies behind the action. But since it makes use of different techniques it can reveal different elements to us—to a large extent, for instance, the undercurrents of conflict between the characters. Also, the plot in a spoken play must be constructed to suit the particular devices of a spoken play while that of an opera must suit the particular device of opera, music. In each case a subject appropriate to opera must obviously sacrifice many elements vital to the spoken play if it is to use its own particular device, music, sensibly and effectively.

Now, when does singing become a believable and, beyond that, a necessary form of expression for a human being? Not when the situation is so unreal to begin with that you no longer mind this ultimate abandonment of reality. Only when it is so filled with life, so cleansed of all extraneous matter, so reduced to one common denominator, and so pointed at the innermost fiber of the actor that he cannot help but express himself by singing and by making music. In other words, the work itself demands music as a release and the performance even more so. The human actions that form the subject of a spoken play or of an opera are not identical. For instance, an important part of a spoken play is given to the weighing of alternatives. In opera this is a preliminary step: one of the alternatives is decided upon. But while in a spoken play the interest turns to the execution (or to the conflicts interfering with the execution) of the decision, in opera the music has just now reached its actual subject: the emotional state behind the decision takes over and manifests itself musically; the inner life of the character is revealed in sound.

The numerous cases in which plays were made into opera librettos do not contradict this theory, provided that by forgoing some of the typical play devices, such as intricate ramifications of the plot, the specific potentialities of the music are made the basis for reshaping the text. One potentiality of the music is, for instance, the simultaneous expression of contrasting emotions, which may turn into sound not only the differing opinions of the various characters but also the accumulated tension in the air.

There are a few plays that have been set to music practically without a cut, word for word. When this is successfully achieved, it proves in some cases the original play contained so much latent music that by raising the threshold to a point where this becomes physically audible, the new version literally seems to be the fulfillment of the original intentions, as with *Pelléas et Mélisande.* In other cases an extensive transformation has taken place, as in *Salome,* where the music strongly illuminates depths which in the play can only be guessed at; this so shifts the emphasis that in their weight and inner content the actions themselves (not merely their artistic representation) are no longer the same, notwithstanding their superficial similarity.

The creative musician hears the music inherent in vital actions, and he fashions it so that others can hear it too. But not in every vital action is there music to be detected. A creative imagination is needed to raise the process to such a meaningful level that the becoming audible of the inner music is not inconsistent with the reality of outer events. If this succeeds, then the elevated expression of music-making seems to be the only proper one. To others who do not possess this creative imagination it takes the work of the composer to make the vital action recognizable in its emotional structure—to make it, one might say, "aurally recognizable." The listener will use the music to confirm the appropriateness of his emotion or to correct it if it is wrong. The composer thus becomes an "educator of emotions." Music lifts the emotions above the threshold of the subconscious, turns the unique experience into a universal one by allowing it to be shared, and gives the inner process a valid form which makes it comprehensible, deepening the shared experience.

Naturally, two composers will tend to hear different music in the same external action because they hear its inner structure differently, because the content is not the same to both. In that case we may well ask whose music is the truer realization and who is interpreting the inner action more correctly.

Voltaire once said, "If something is too stupid to be said, then let it be sung." We might reverse this dictum by saying; "Something can be sung only when the verbal expression is no longer adequate to give shape to the essential element of the action."

Since not everything that happens in the course of a plot contains music, the melodic outpouring and the continuous rhythmic involvement of the orchestra should take over only at the point where the tension onstage has become so concentrated that music is the only release. For the remainder of the time the action may be carried by unaccompanied pantomime, spoken dialogue, or the various forms of recitative. It was one of the fatal errors of the Wagner succession that they denied this condition for the taking over of the music and made an ideal of "through-composition." If this ideal can exist at all, the realization of it lies with the poet (who in the case of Wagner obviously was also the composer); he must create a drama which from beginning to end is soaked with inner music. But what happened to be true of *Tristan* does not necessarily hold for other subjects.

We can put this all together as follows: That acting human beings should express themselves through singing is not inconsistent, and is even necessary, if the action is planned to compel emotional release in singing and if it provides space for the unfolding of inner experiences. It can be done when the underlying human drives are condensed to such a degree that they must be transformed into music in order to be perceived and understood. In this situation the action is lifted above the realm of everyday life by intensification, not removed from reality by absurdity.

Now, if a human being is more positive in his intentions and sensibilities than other human beings, capable of finding musical expression for his inner experiences, and thereby making clear to the listener what otherwise could only be deduced or surmised, why should it be said that this human being is no longer a human being? Should the behavior of someone who is shown as completely possessed by an idea not be believable? Should his inner animation relieve him of the necessity to convince the spectator of his live existence or to deal with realities in a real fashion —the very same realities that have come about as a result of his inner experiences? The roots of his sensibilities lie in reality, and reality is his goal, even if his reach is exceeding his grasp. Should he, while striving toward his goal, driven by his will, be allowed to appear helpless? Should he be unconscious of what is going on around him, unaware that he is even expressing his feelings, or perhaps—let us be honest—preoccupied with technical difficulties?

The relationship between singing and reality in opera can be made believable only when the singer achieves the compatible union of two factors within himself:

1. The ability to portray correctly the external action in a situation which has been so reduced to its essence as to make singing possible, and so intensified as to make it necessary.
2. Complete absorption in the content that drives him to sing.

It is not sufficient for the creators to have intensified the situation to such a degree, and to have charged the characters with so much energy, as to make music an absolutely necessary means of expression. If the singer cannot make the character's viewpoint his own and is not able to generate these intensities within himself, then he can never convince the audience that his singing is anything more than a convention which is pleasing to the ear. The singer has it in his power to determine whether operagoers must make do with a performance that sounds good but is dramatically incomprehensible (even though it obeys the rules of craftsmanship) or whether they are to learn something about their own lives.

Our principles are summarized in the term "music theater," as it has been coined at the Komische Oper under its founder and head, Walter Felsenstein. They are very simple and can be reduced to one basic law: that of the truthfulness of the action. The singer must not do anything at the command of somebody else, whether it is the composer, the librettist, the conductor, or the stage director. He must produce everything, including his own singing, by himself, as a necessary expression of his inner state, as a necessary projection of his striving, and as a necessary reaction to the actions of his partners. One must not gain the impression for one single moment that he could have expressed himself differently, with other words or other sounds. This presupposes that he has made the intentions of the composer and the author completely his own; it also presupposes that singer, conductor, and stage director are completely in accord with one another. During the performance the singer should not be the executant but, as it were, the creator. Therefore it must not seem that the composer chose a certain form arbitrarily and for its own sake; rather this form must appear to be the inevitable and spontaneous result of the situation between the characters on the stage at a given moment.

The simplicity of this principle distinguishes music theater from the production routine of "traditional opera," in which there is a tug-of-war between different responsibilities—between so-called stylistic requirements on one side, and practical obstacles that have to be taken into account on the other.

Music theater is the opposite of "singing with expression and also acting." Precisely this juxtaposition of singing and acting is the root of all evil in many opera performances, in spite of "good stage direction." In music theater, the music is not something that already exists, into which the singer feels his way as he sings it: he felt his way into the music during preparation, making it his own, and now he seems to produce it himself. Our method of work therefore moves in reverse to that of the composer's: from the human origin to the sound. We have now arrived at a fundamental rule, and also at the secret of the impact of a performance based on music theater principles: the singer must "anticipate" the music. He is to produce not only his own singing but also (seemingly) the playing of the orchestra, to the extent that it is the expression of his own emotion. Only when the emotion already exists in the singer, or when he has initiated an action, does the orchestra join him and turn the emotion or action into its own sound. The spectator has observed the origin of the process, and then the orchestra confirms the correctness of his feeling; the fixation into orchestral sound makes the process irreversible. He has been guided in a certain direction by his visual impression, then there is a moment of tension, and now, in his inner ear as it were, a sound is produced that is in accord with his feelings.

Performing in the reverse order (first the sound, then the action) may make the singer look funny, as if he had been startled by the orchestra and is now quickly trying to furnish the necessary action, or, if this is not the case, may create the impression of a marionette being manipulated by the music. The result appears as a kind of fatalism. Only the music theater portrays man as acting freely and shows that the world can be changed.

The main tower of strength in our work is the conductor. It is in his hands to determine whether the performance will be or will not be music theater, and the most beautiful stage direction comes to naught if he has not made the conception his own. Music theater means the dethronement of the podium dictator. It books no guest appearances of star conductors, nor does it assign to the conductor the role of a mere accompanist. In unison with the impulses of the stage, from the well-attuned and carefully balanced efforts of the individual performers and through creative execution of the will of the composer, he shapes the unbroken line of the theatrical happening.

Music theater also opposes the concept of the star stage director. Rather, it establishes the thinking, performing artist who transforms himself into the character he portrays; to him the stage director is only a helper, a mirror to tell him whether his interpretation is sufficiently clear and intelligible to the spectator, an arranger and coordinator who sees the individual in relation to the total effect and puts the details together into a harmonious entity.

The way from salesman of vocal skills to inspired re-creator of the music, ruling the stage but still serving the work, is long and arduous. Only he is qualified who thinks no more about superficial effects, vocal and otherwise, and remains but a faithful servant of the music theater, of the story and its message.

Finally, one word about our own situation, which confronts us with the difficult task of applying the principles of the music theater to the day-to-day reality of a routined (and sometimes overroutined) theatrical organization. The music theater needs works that are conceived in accordance with its rules—the masterworks of Mozart and Verdi, for example. But what should one do with operas lacking in the qualities we require—with self-aggrandizement in the music, flaws in the plot, and implausible developments in human conflicts? One should not capitulate before these works, not try to create out of their negative qualities a principle of abstract antitheater, but approach them from their most positive side and, if at all possible, do something to overcome their weaknesses.

By the same token it is impossible to fill every part with a performer who can transform himself perfectly into the role. When a singer cannot do this, rather than yield and renounce our ideals entirely, we must still try to lead him as close to it as possible. This approach will result in more credibility than if, accepting the limitations of what can be achieved, we were to deny from the outset our goal of truthfulness.

19

Dramaturgy in the Music Theater

by Stephan Stompor

(Stage director by training and professional background, Stephan Stompor is a member of the dramaturgic staff of the Komische Oper; he has been in that capacity almost since the inception of the operation. The following article, published in 1955 in *Theater der Zeit,* Berlin, offers an unusual insight into the preparations that went into Felsenstein's staging of *The Magic Flute.*)

To interpret a work according to the principles of the music theater, two complex tasks are of overriding importance: discovering the action in the music to permit the translation of the score into a living, believable scenic occurrence, and clarifying the relationship of the spiritual and dramatic conception to the visual shape of the production. Just as it is for any worthwhile staging of a spoken play, the starting point for the preparation of a musical work is an analysis of its spiritual content. This is naturally based on the premise that we accept the piece as a dramatic work of art which in the presentation of gripping and fascinating events shows the image of man in its entire complexity, tells the truth about life, and awakens perception and even transformation in the spectator. It goes without saying that we also try to make our productions pleasurable and entertaining.

In many musical works the message is not presented as clearly as in most spoken plays because the coordination between musical form and dramatic requirements has not always been completely successful. Not all composers have the dramatic talent of Mozart and Verdi, and many of them have made concessions to public taste. And in many works the dramatic content has suffered in the past through inadequate rendition, sometimes to the point of becoming unintelligible.

Mozart's *Magic Flute* is a classic example of this. The new staging of the work by Walter Felsenstein at the Komische Oper in Berlin has demonstrated clearly to what extent the spiritual message of the music has been ignored in the past. This production is so wonderfully instructive, because of its thoroughly and consistently thought-out dramatic and scenic conception, that one can deduce from it many of the challenges in the work of a music theater which meets today's demands.

It is true that the age when musical numbers from other operas were thoughtlessly interpolated in this work lies far behind us; even so, do not many people still retain the idea that although the music of *The Magic Flute* is marvelous, the action is fairly primitive and senselessly patched together? The work has often been interpreted as Mozart's statement of faith in humanity, expressing his belief in the victory of good over evil and presenting in the guise of a fairy tale the humanistic ideals of a rising citizenry during the time of the French Revolution. Yet the attempt to translate this theoretical knowledge into a moving, intelligible theatrical experience has hardly ever been successful. In most cases the producer has adhered to the traditional clichés, dating back to the time when audiences, too lazy to think or to receive new experiences and without particular interest in discovering spiritual content on the musical stage, wished merely to hear a sequence of familiar, beautiful musical numbers, and when many singers had grown accustomed to reproducing memorized notes, under the conductor's supervision, without bothering to think about the meaning of the words. Under these circumstances the content could not impress the spectators because they simply did not understand it. On the other hand, many people who witnessed

Felsenstein's production said that only now were they able to understand what *The Magic Flute* was all about, and that for the first time they had realized and fully absorbed the meaning of this "fairy tale" in all its proximity to life.

It is worthwhile to examine some of the factors that caused this production to be such a profound and lasting experience. Surely, the insight into the music theater gained from this can logically be transferred to the scenic and musical processing of any other work.

In this examination the lines of observation always lead back to one basic point: the conception is so deeply and clearly thought out that all characters, actions, and visual elements are completely integrated. This illustrates the fact that the stage director needs to be not only an expert psychologist, as well as an artistic and, for the musical stage, a highly musical person; he must also be a clear dramatic thinker. Here we have not one of the usual productions, but a reinterpretation of *The Magic Flute* in terms of the present, an attempt to make it intelligible and to bring it closer to the audience. We see the confrontation between light and darkness, the trials of the human being in this confrontation, and the heartwarming victory of the new over the decayed and evil. All this has been shaped into dramatic action, with an incredible closeness to life, and only now does Mozart's music, as the medium of the exalted ideas of humanity, take on its true meaning and its full power of conviction.

Two functions of the stage director seem to me worthy of special emphasis. First, he must make a dramatic work intelligible (this requires mainly a consistent, realistic development of the action and a clear profiling of the characters and their relations with each other, as well as an unmistakable representation of the places of action); second, he must interpret the content of the work for the spectator as a personal confession, yet one that is valid in terms of our time. In order to do this he must imbue the presentation with his knowledge, his musicianship, and the full range of his sensitivity. Felsenstein has handled both of these jobs admirably. To perceive the inner substance—which, after all, in an opera is expressed not merely in the text—and to give it scenic form, utilizing all available means: that is how one might briefly define the task of the modern stage director. Both in relation to the spiritual preparation and to the practical work during rehearsals, a number of chores become incumbent upon him.

The basis of the director's work, according to the music theater, is in every case the musical and dramatic analysis of the work, which I shall describe more fully further on. The director and all the participants in a production can obtain new perspectives by studying the lives and other works of the composer and librettist, as well as letters and other written communications, reports from contemporaries, and so on. It is also stimulating and important to study the historic conditions surrounding the creative efforts of the composer, the chronology of the work's origin, the time and environment in which the action takes place, corresponding pictorial representations, and, most of all, the related literary documents, both factual and fictional. All these resources were utilized in the process of staging *The Magic Flute* at the Berlin Komische Oper, particularly the discoveries of the Viennese experts Egon Komorzynski and Otto Rommel, who brought a new point of view to the study of Mozart's opera. Contrary to the widely accepted idea that *The Magic Flute* is an opera written by Schikaneder and Mozart without much thought and with a "break" in the action, Komorzynski and Rommel call attention to the smoothly joined unity of text and music; they focus the correct light on the personality of Schikaneder as a progressive theater expert, and they see the work not only as Mozart's testament to mankind but also as the climax of Schikaneder's creative endeavor.

On the basis of these studies and adhering to a scholarly picture of Mozart, it was possible to present the opera, even in its most delicate nuances, as a gripping drama and as a consistent, seamless unity. Guided by the work itself and by the spirit of

Mozart's music, the dramatic proceedings were illuminated and brought to life without intellectualizing and artificiality, and certainly without doing violence to the music. Even the first step, the opening of a few traditional cuts in the dialogue, resulted in new perspectives on the motivation, helping also to supplement the exposition and to supply connecting links in the action heretofore not utilized. Thus every incident was meaningfully related to the underlying theme of the work—the triumph of love, kindness, will power, and spirituality over arrogance, superstition, and lust for power, this being the postulate of an epoch in which the longing for spirituality, happiness, and peace determines the actions of all men. And in spite of the elements of fantasy, the theme acquired a dramatic form that was real and directly related to life.

The action of *The Magic Flute* is set into a great and significant context which can be felt clearly and immediately, but also indirectly, in the scenic rendition. Let us isolate a few incidents which have almost always remained obscure or which have been thoughtlessly passed over. Until now the three spirits were regarded as belonging to Sarastro's sphere, and a dramatic contradiction was seen in the superficially peculiar fact that the ladies, being the deputies of the Queen of the Night, entrust Tamino and Papageno to the spirits' guidance (therefore, according to tradition, to the followers of Sarastro), even giving the two men the magic flute and magic bells to protect them from mishaps. Felsenstein, however, sees the function of the three spirits in accordance with the dramatic development: neither do they belong to Sarastro nor are they under the sway of the Queen of the Night; they intervene in the action as neutral genii, although they are dedicated to assisting the good. The queen believes that she can make use of them to implement her lust for power (in reality the spirits lead Tamino and Papageno into the paths of virtue). Visually, the neutrality of the spirits is expressed by the fact that they always appear on a cloud carriage, on which they soar away again after completing a definite action.

A further confirmation of the "break" in the action was seen in the circumstance that Sarastro keeps Monostatos the Moor in his service; this was explained as a remnant left from the first version of the work, in which allegedly the queen was shown as a kind fairy and Sarastro as an evil sorcerer. In the present staging the character of Monostatos is thoroughly reinterpreted. Until now he has always been, in gesture, costume, and makeup, malicious and lecherous perhaps, but basically a cliché-comical black man: it was hardly believable that Sarastro would honor him with his confidence and entrust to him the important duty of guarding Pamina. In Felsenstein's version Monostatos has become a strong personality. We witness the almost tragic conflict between his loyalty to Sarastro and his eagerness to please him, on one hand, and his lust for Pamina—a by-product of the Moor's daily encounters with the beautiful girl—and his resulting fear of Sarastro on the other. We sense that he is disposed to commit bad deeds but that he is not innately evil; circumstances force him into it (in this case, being given a task beyond his limitations). This sense of inadequacy also explains his domineering attitude toward Pamina and the slaves: he is the only black person among whites. Of course, one could continue by asking, for instance, how Monostatos became a servant of Sarastro and what the social position of slaves in the realm of the Initiates might be.* Undoubtedly these questions came up during rehearsals and were properly answered.

Even Pamina's frustrated attempt to flee and Sarastro's words "Zur Liebe will ich dich nicht zwingen, doch geb' ich dir die Freiheit nicht"** have always been interpreted as a confirmation of the "break" in the action. Similarly, the first aria of the Queen of the Night has been viewed as an expression of genuine moth-

*I remember reading in a rehearsal report that Felsenstein had told his cast Monostatos was a Nubian prince who had been given to Sarastro as a prisoner of war—that he had to perform menial duties against which he rebelled, and which sometimes made him lose control. Ed.

**"I do not wish to force you to love, yet I shall not give you your freedom."

erly sadness over the loss of her daughter; its sharp contrast to the actions of the queen in the second act were always attributed to changes made later in the libretto. In Felsenstein's staging even the queen's first aria appears as the expression of her ruthless ambition, the motherly sadness becoming a tactical weapon for the attainment of her goal and consequently strongly exaggerated. This is in accord with the dramatic function of the queen in the scenario, and with the conception on which this production is based. Even the music of both arias employs similar stylistic devices, borrowed from *opera seria,* pointing up their similar character. The reason for removing Pamina from her mother's sphere of influence has been explained and set into a larger context by the assumption that Pamina's father had begged Sarastro to take the girl under his protection in order to have her marry Tamino later. Pamina does not know all that; she senses only the pain of separation from her mother and her home, and a certain severity on the part of Sarastro (behind which, however, a deep affection for the girl lies concealed). The relationship between Sarastro and Pamina thereby appears in a new light, and Sarastro's words quoted above as well as Pamina's attempt to flee are motivated.*

On the basis of this conception it was possible to crystallize many elements of the action that had remained obscure until now, and to present Mozart's masterwork as a unified dramatic entity.

*See *Why Does Pamina Flee?* on page 65.

20

Set Designer for the Music Theater

by Rudolf Heinrich

(Associated with the Komische Oper for many years as one of its foremost designers, Rudolf Heinrich has been solely responsible for the sets and costumes of such famous Felsenstein productions as *Traviata, Otello, Hoffmann, Midsummer Night's Dream,* and Janáček's *Sly Little Vixen.* The following article was published in 1957 in *10 Jahre Komische Oper Berlin.* In the United States Mr. Heinrich is known for his work with the Metropolitan and Santa Fe Operas.)

It does not seem necessary to write here about the details of set designing, the technical conditions and the possibilities, since these are of direct interest only to a small circle of experts. The results of our work can be seen in the theater every evening.

Today it seems obvious, at least theoretically, that the set designer is a dramatic collaborator in the visual part of the production. For that reason it is important to show how he must make his choice between "fine arts" and "theater."

As the youngest of the classical forms of the European theater, opera has always engendered the most extreme reactions. They range from rapturous enthusiasm to total rejection, the latter coming from the defenders of pure aestheticism, who cannot seem to fit the genre into their rules. However, opera is alive in spite of that, and even today still enjoys a mysterious popularity. It has created its own artistic place and has become valid in its own right, not subject to a purely aesthetic evaluation. The substance of an opera therefore cannot be made visible simply by following the prevailing rules of taste of the period but only by meeting the internal requirements of the work itself. All genuine music dramas contain their own laws of realization and these laws, in the works that appeal to us today, grow out of the relevance of the drama to the human being. Thus man, the measure of all things, becomes (through the actor) the measure of form and content for the visual occurrence onstage. Transformation of the actor through costume and makeup may serve only one purpose: to reinforce the fundamental characteristics of his role; any other use of costume and makeup (for their pictorial value) dehumanizes him. He remains connected with the drama only as a manifestation of taste.

This very thing, however, happens everywhere. It springs from the desire of set designers to create a "pure" theatrical image, as a parallel to the striving of all arts to "purify" themselves of thematic "deadweight," the goal being total abstraction. In Paris, for instance, people obviously had become accustomed to pictorial abstractions paralleling the action on the stage. Our set of *The Sly Little Vixen* therefore created a strange impression, as we can see by the criticism of Jacques Bourgeois in *L'Art:* "There is nothing else left to us except to silence our good French taste, and to accept the *Vixen* from Berlin in its total unity of form and content, which is the best indication of an artistic success."

In order to accomplish this unity of form and content, any means is permissible. Thus it is possible, in a work that requires no pinpointing of time and place—for instance, *The Wise Maiden* by Orff—to let the drama come into being merely through the relations between human beings whose characterizations have been established by gesture and costume and even, for the sake of that effect, forgo painting a broader picture by means of illusionary devices.

The stage design of *The Magic Flute* was a totally different problem. The various basic elements of the work had to be tied into a cheerful unity without giving up their independence. Just as the theme grew out of many varied sources, mostly Oriental, similarly the cultures of the countries alluded to had to be represented wherever a sensible opportunity arose. To connect all these parts we used a frame of baroque architecture, whose bright and outgoing festivity was meant to create the atmosphere of the homeland of the composer and librettist; it was an attempt to give the "artistic fairy tale" an "artistic space" in which to unfold.

The principles of the music theater can be reaffirmed by the example of Janáček's *Sly Little Vixen.* The work lay before us without any model or tradition to follow. It seemed to be a fairy tale—a fable—but we soon recognized that it is neither; it represents a poetic but precise realism in which animals and human beings must be able to exist side by side. To produce a forest that meets these requirements is a punishment for a modern stage designer. Our trust in the old, purely pictorial theatrical devices has been demolished, and we remember their dust-covered effect with terror. It will be understandable that at first the fear of competition with the perfection of nature made us consider merely "hinting" at objects in an intelligible formal language, in the hope that the spectators themselves might fill in the necessary details. Yet here again the work itself forced us to give up this idea. There is an unbroken chain, starting with the burdened schoolteacher, going on to the impetuous forester, to the crowd of petty, envious villagers, to Terynka, free as an animal, close in spirit to the vixen, and finally to the grouchy animals of the forest, such as the badger and the owl, and the sunny, short-lived forest insects. Here the chain could not be broken if one wanted to keep faith with Janáček's music. This entire throng must find shelter and nutrition in the forest. Trees, bark, moss, cracks and fissures, roots and ferns had to be there, at least as *pars pro toto.* This was the starting point of the *Vixen* forest. It is not surprising that aesthetes who strongly favor the so-called modern style use "naturalism" as a demeaning epithet to defend their viewpoint. The public and most of the critics, however, seem to have understood completely what had to be done in this work. A critic in Wiesbaden wrote: "Within this naturalism a mysterious change of quality takes place, such as we know it from the paintings of Caravaggio and Vermeer. It is the privilege of art, in rare moments, to condense physical reality to a point at which it transforms itself into the spiritual without losing its substance."

Without wishing to detract from the good luck that blessed this production, I will say that it is probably not the "rare moments" but the attitude that makes the transformation possible: with all our desire for individual freedom to feel our way into a work and its situations, we still wish to arrive at forms that are universally comprehensible. For without the clear perceptibility of its dramatic function, every object onstage is like an actor who does not know his role. During a discussion in Paris the statement was made that to strive for universal intelligibility was "inartistic." Art was said to be subjective interpretation, responsible only to itself. As an answer, it would be proper to quote Hegel: "Whoever invokes his feelings, his inner oracle, can no longer relate to anyone who does not agree with him; in effect, he is declaring that he has nothing to say to the person who does not find and feel the same within himself. In other words, he is trampling on the very basis of humanity, since it is the nature of humanity to strive for harmony with others."

Perhaps one might say that *Vixen* is an exceptional case, and that other productions of the Komische Oper are not as different visually from productions elsewhere. Why should they be? Sets that used to be considered shocking experiments, and were usually oriented more to the fine arts than to the theater, have long since lost their excitement. Since these attempt to be striking for the sake of effect only, they will not bow to a dramatic obligation. We are forced to realize that even today's painting cannot help us very much, since most of it keeps its distance from the human form and, following its true nature, is antidramatic. The task of the set designer in the music theater is therefore more one of a "writer," who labels the unnamed scenic objects and makes them materially visible. We believe in the diversity of this realistic principle; every day can bring new experiences and there will be fresh points of view which will express more clearly what must be said. We need not be in fear of confining ourselves too closely. If one duty of art is to help man and to liberate him, this is the only way in which it can be done in the theater. For man can find freedom not in fleeing from reality but in loving it and mastering it. It is only within the boundaries of reality that a human drama becomes possible.

21

The New *Traviata*

by Siegfried Melchinger

(A review of Felsenstein's staging of *La Traviata* at the Hamburg State Opera* which appeared in the *Stuttgarter Zeitung* of February 16, 1960. Siegfried Melchinger is an outstanding authority on theater and opera in Germany, and an expert on Felsenstein's work.)

It is a sign of our times that we distrust the traditional and oppose it in a work of art with a show of energy that is tinged perhaps with jealousy. In this spirit we took a trip to Hamburg, not in order to experience a perfect opera performance at the State Opera, but rather to see a *Traviata* such as we had never seen before. We knew this could be expected of Walter Felsenstein, who had staged it. This passionate lover of accuracy has realized that an operatic presentation can have vitality only when the performer's imagination is creatively engaged, which means that everything settled on a work in the course of many performances, out of a more or less cherished routine, must be removed. Nothing tends more to slovenliness than the popular favorites and we, the recipients, also tend to enjoy them in a slovenly fashion. When a fanatic like Toscanini, Felsenstein, or Callas turns to *Traviata*, this whole situation changes. "Bold to the utmost" was what Verdi wanted of the work. Felsenstein gave it back its birthright.

*See the interview with Rolf Liebermann on page 111.

You can listen to the overture leaning back comfortably in your upholstered chair; it will always strike you as a piece of music beautifully put together, a sequence of expressive melodies, a staple of all open-air concerts at health resorts. Yet when Verdi wrote it, he chose as the beginning the melody of death (which in the opera itself returns only once, at the death of Violetta), because he knew that although this was to be an opera about love, as all operas were in those happier days, it was to be at the same time an opera about death. "Ultimately, is not everything in life death? What is permanent?" he wrote at that time to Clarina.*

Felsenstein took quite seriously the intention expressed in the overture. He had his masterly young designer, Rudolf Heinrich, build him a courtyard of black columns in which to enclose the events. A stark and gloomy tomb, the visualization of the rhythm of trombone and tuba blasts with which Verdi (and not only in *Traviata*) announces the arrival of death.

Meanwhile, there is the roar of festivity of the first act. Dark red draperies, red and gold screens which are suddenly pulled aside to reveal supper tables covered in dazzling white, a flock of liveried servants dashing out, ready to pour champagne. Excellent chorus direction, you say to yourself, but you are already aware that certain features emerge from the basic mood of this festivity and certain trends are set. Alfredo intones the Drinking Song—he is a smiling, nature-loving type of tenor—and all eyes are directed toward Violetta, the "traviata," the fallen one, who in turn stares at this apparition from another world, much to the irritation of her partner, the baron.

The attention focuses on Violetta and Alfredo. Now they are alone. Violetta has suffered the first attack of her disease; this seems to increase her uneasiness. In evident disgust she lets the guests dance by her, so that they may hurry home and catch some sleep before the next party. Alfredo's song echoes in her ear and turns into a terrible seduction. She gulps the champagne down

*The reference is to Countess Clarina Maffei, Verdi's lifelong friend and correspondent. Ed.

and throws herself into the coloraturas to forget everything, as if she had a premonition of the end that is bound to come if she follows the voice. The black columns.

In the second scene, in which the columns have been transformed into a forest of silver pines, the emissary of fate must be presented. I could not agree with Felsenstein on the character of the elder Germont, whom he views critically and depicts as a narrow-minded bourgeois, with an almost peasantlike brutality. This can be justified: what Alfredo's father demands is certainly brutal. It is also in accord with Verdi's own life: exactly at that time he was living "illegitimately" with his mistress, and for that reason had to submit to all kinds of insult; in addition, he had chosen this daring subject in order to give vent to his hatred for "clerics, monks, and hypocrites."

However, is it possible to make this jibe with the music that Verdi wrote for Germont *père?* The hackneyed, abused aria remains one of his noblest inspirations. It is unthinkable that a thick-skinned dullard would produce such melodies. If, however, Verdi gave him these melodies to sing, then the composer must have put aside here his condemnation of society's moral standards. And I feel that this is a crucial point. *La Traviata* can still move us nowadays because, in spite of all statements to the contrary, the problem of love—marriage versus illicit love—is as timely now as it was then. Verdi's opinion of wantonness is attested to by his music. One need merely compare the Allegro brillante of the demimondain feasts in *Traviata* with a cancan by Offenbach. And the fact that the image of the "pudica vergine," the modest virgin, reappears in Violetta's last song before her death, unmistakably reminding us of the "figlia pura" for whose sake she had left Alfredo—this points in the same direction. Seen in that light, the illness gives the drama momentum: it is the consequence of wantonness. "Parigi noi lasceremo" (We shall leave Paris) are the words in the last duet of the dying girl. Evidently she had already left Paris in the second scene; perhaps she might be cured in the country air. But she must go back to the past that has tainted her, and this means, as she clearly says herself, back to the disease, and to death.

The third scene (which occurs, unfortunately, after a misplaced intermission; Verdi had intended this scene as a finale to the second scene) left no room for such deliberations. It was of a gloomy, oppressive kind of beauty. Again the columns, but this time encompassing more emptiness than in the first scene. A slanted ceiling, draped with a huge scarf, candelabra and chaises longues, all in silver and black. Masquerade. Carnival.

The choruses of Gypsies and toreadors (foolishly often presented as a ballet divertissement) showing the entrance and dance of masked guests. In the upstage area, protruding diagonally onto the scene, an open staircase, descending gradually from the base of the columns, with black and silver railing. There Violetta appeared—as soon as Alfredo had sat down with the card players—on the arm of her baron, in a wine red gown. It was an eerie, unforgettable moment. Later, on the same staircase, after Alfredo had finished with his scene of scandal, Germont *père* appeared in overcoat and top hat, a specter against whom the accusation for the catastrophe was directed.

In the play by Dumas you may distrust the blatant melodrama of this act. In Verdi's opera it is no longer suspect, provided that the emotion-charged tension of the music is staged as Felsenstein does it. Violetta's anxiously ascending melody during the card game seemed almost geometrically placed into the action, as did the image presented by her in the finale, which offered a pale and searing premonition of the last act.

That act was dominated by the singer, Melitta Muszely. Nestled into the chair, with her profile turned toward the doctor, she reminded you of Edvard Munch's *Sick Girl* (which unquestionably was not intentional, but simply a result of the related situation). Her glance in the mirror after the reading of the letter, the tearless despair over her own decline, brought back the feelings of anxiety which in the second scene had justified the decision of renunciation: what will happen when youth and beauty are gone, when I may still love Alfredo but he cannot love me any longer? And what will happen now that he has promised to return to me and he finds me like this? The filigree head of this Violetta was like a broken blossom on a long stem; and when she slipped out of Alfredo's embrace to don her cape—"and now to church"—the tottering of illness turned into a dance of death in which she seemed to transform herself into an angel. And this music! Heaven and hell, the deathly futility of life, and our transfiguration when the suffering is over, when there is nothing more to suffer. Who could be ashamed of tears at this moment?

Bold to the utmost, true to the utmost: the painful birth of beauty. Verdi's work, just as it was on the first day of its existence.

22

The Stage Director Walter Felsenstein

by Horst Koegler

(Horst Koegler is one of West Germany's leading music critics, known also for his contributions to the English magazine *Opera.* This article appeared in *Der Monat* in 1958.)

Felsenstein succeeds in having his singing actors completely identify with their roles. He also makes absolutely sure that they renounce all set operatic patterns, all clichés of acting, all stereotyped routines, and all interpolated gags heretofore considered indispensable. He knows how to free his singers from the fear of speaking dialogue (I would not go so far as to say that the lines sound as if they were spoken by real actors, but, when delivered by Felsenstein's performers, they invariably sound more *significant*), and liberates them also from the need of visual contact with the conductor. His work with the performer is initially nothing but a removal, layer by layer, of the commonplace interpretation of a role acquired either at the conservatory or during earlier theater experience. He leads the performer away from a prefabricated general conception to a unique characterization which, feature by feature, he turns into a realistic portrait. In Felsenstein's production of *Carmen,* every smuggler appears in Lillas Pastia's tavern as a clearly differentiated type, and Pastia himself is a highly individualized arch-scoundrel.

Felsenstein's remarkable direction of individuals is apparent in the way his artists seem to radiate space around them, creating an atmosphere for each character, not only when it is "their turn," and they have something to say or sing, but even when they stand silent. They produce their own three-dimensional living space, which often is much more real than the one created by the set designer.

For instance, the way Felsenstein makes his people walk! How the smugglers in *Carmen* walk—not the usual careless strolling over elevations and staircases, but breakneck feats of mountain climbing, the movement of which carries over into the cautious groping for the ground underfoot when they walk in the tavern. What a world of difference between their walk and that of the peasant Krushina in *The Bartered Bride,* who swaggers in long, mighty strides, as if to say, "This is my land, and woe to him who should try to take it away from me!" Make no mistake about it, however: Felsenstein does not invent steps to fit the music, but rather steps and gestures that fit each character in a given situation. It is wrong to say that he directs in choreographic movements; he does that only occasionally, when there is music without singing, such as in Orff's *Die Kluge (The Wise Maiden)* where he has the musicians move in a way that is vaguely reminiscent of Moorish dances, or in the *Figaro* procession in the finale of Act III, which he allows to unfold with the solemn gravity of a Spanish court ritual. It should also be mentioned here with what incredible skill Felsenstein integrates a seemingly superfluous ballet into the opera action, how he leads from one element into another, or lets one result from another, as if this were the most natural thing in the world (even though he rightly dispenses with the ballet-divertissement in the last act of *Carmen*).

Felsenstein always has stressed the fact that he takes great pains to bring his characters to life, and actually I cannot think of any director of the musical theater who knows how to "animate" his performers in the same way. He has particular success with female roles, which radiate so much purity, kindness, warm sensitivity, and loving compassion that even jaded theatergoers admit to suffering tortures with Micaela, Agathe *(Freischütz)*, Mařenka *(Bartered Bride)*, and Pamina. But a number of male roles also remain firmly imprinted on one's memory: the dazed, uncomprehending Don José, the lovably helpless Vashek in *Bartered Bride*, who literally stutters from an overflowing heart, and of course Papageno. Two more roles need to be mentioned specifically: Falstaff, and the noise-shy Sir Morosus in Strauss's *The Silent Woman*. When these two persons philosophize on the world and on mankind with the smiling wisdom of old age, then such a wave of heartfelt humanity—the knowledge and acceptance, even sanction, of all imperfections—inundates the audience that it overwhelms the most critical spectator.

Felsenstein's ability to bring his characters to life is most triumphantly evident in the great crowd scenes. What he can accomplish with choristers is something one must see to believe. He calls them "chorus soloists" *(Chorsolisten)*; they are not anonymous members of a multitude but carefully shaped individuals. Take the variety of different, not to say heterogeneous, types to be found at the party of Prince Orlofsky, which is a rendezvous of the entire aristocracy on the Danube. And again it is necessary to name *Carmen*. How the passionate furioso of this chorus opera develops step by step, from a few lazy Sevillian burghers and a few bored soldiers in the beginning to the theatrical eruption of unparalleled sensuous intoxication in the last act, when all of Seville is gathered in front of the bullfight arena, and how this continues to build up! After seemingly the last summit has been reached with the entrance of the toreador, Felsenstein adds still a final accent by including the spectators sitting in the arena, who follow the bullfight with the utmost concentration, as a visual counterpoint to the quarrel of Carmen and José taking place in the foreground. This is an unforgettable tour de force.

And how realistically profiled these people are! Your nose seems to sense the sweat, the dust, the aroma of oil, the pungent odor of the stables, and the stench blowing over from the Guadalquivir. Equally unforgettable is the jubilation of the entire population of the village in *Bartered Bride* when the traveling circus (with real circus performers) pitches its tent on the meadow, from which you can see the Bohemian fields overflowing with ripe grain. All this is so contagious in its Dionysian joy of living that you feel like jumping up from your orchestra seat to join the crowd on the stage. (How cleverly Felsenstein manages to take advantage of this unconscious urge of the audience by having actors enter from the auditorium!) And again you notice that he stages chorus scenes dreaded by every opera stage director—the song of the bridesmaids and the hunters' chorus in *Freischütz,* the students' chorus in *Tales of Hoffmann*—with such freshness that you have the sensation of being present at the world premiere.

One more word about Felsenstein as a stage technician. Part of his liberation of the music theater from opera clichés consists of doing away with the traditional props. For example, he deprives Kecal of his customary umbrella, but to replace the laughs lost this way he provides so many original nuances that in the end Kecal emerges as a much funnier figure. Generally, Felsenstein is not at a loss for gags, but he never uses them for their own sake. And time and again he shows himself to be a master of comic movement, whether it is in the staging of *The Wise Maiden,* the movement of the opera troupe in *The Silent Woman,* the dance of the Moors in *Magic Flute,* or the round of the chickens in Janáček's *Sly Little Vixen.* You can sense the joy with which he plunges into a scene of movement—for instance, when there are duels to be fought. The combat between Hoffmann and Schlemihl comes across the footlights as a fully realistic life-and-death struggle.

23

Random Notes Taken During a Felsenstein Seminar

by Peter Paul Fuchs

(From April 30 until May 2, 1971, Felsenstein offered a seminar at Boston University for opera professionals and educators invited from all over the United States. I attended as an ordinary participant, but was soon pressed into service as an interpreter for Felsenstein. Most of the following notes were taken while listening to Felsenstein address the audience in German, and translating his words into English for the benefit of the audience. Considering this, I cannot claim that they are precise, but I do hope they will reveal some pertinent facts not encountered in his writings.

Many of Felsenstein's remarks were of a general nature. But he also spent several hours each with a soprano on the staging of Violetta's recitative "E strano," and with a baritone on Iago's *Credo* from *Otello.*)

1. GENERAL REMARKS

Felsenstein believes in the absolute truth of the stage action. In order to perform an action truthfully, the actor must attempt it first according to his own personality, *not* trying to be the character. He should concentrate on the basic emotion of the action involved—love, hate, fear, disgust, and so on. He should practice this emotion until he can feel it wholeheartedly, and until it appears genuine to the spectator. This can be accomplished by verbalizing the action in various ways, not necessarily with words belonging to the play itself. If the action is directed toward a specific person, particularly toward somebody who is absent, then this person must be clearly visualized by the actor.

* *

There are monologues of contemplation and of inspiration. A monologue of contemplation yields results that emerge gradually, a product of thought. A monologue of inspiration produces results in sudden flashes that overpower the character and leave him no time for thought.

* *

Perhaps Felsenstein's most important principle concerns the coordination of music and acting: the actor must not *follow* the music but must *release* it, meaning he must provide the occasion for the music to happen. This requires that each action be started a beat or two ahead of its music. Needless to say, in order to do it correctly the singing actor must be thoroughly familiar with the melodic and rhythmic structure of the score.

If, however, the singing actor merely "synchronizes" his movements with the music, as happens so often, he gives the effect of actually falling behind the music; he also appears to be following it mechanically, rather than making it come alive through his own inspiration.

It is very important for the singing actor to absorb the feeling of the music completely, in his body and in his facial expression. He must never drop his intensity or make "pauses" of expression between sentences. Felsenstein reports that at the Komische Oper in Berlin the rehearsal accompanists are trained to watch the action during rehearsals very closely. The moment a singer performs an action with an unsuitable expression, the accompanist immediately falsifies the expression of his playing accordingly, to make the singer aware of his mistake.

* *

Felsenstein's description of the process of the actor's getting into character: the first stage is to become acquainted with the objectives. The actor must study the entire background carefully, be fully aware of the physical and psychological situation on which a scene is based, and then examine the various emotional and intellectual components of the action.

In the second stage, the actor must completely abandon himself to the emotions. They must become part of him, and he must drive himself to the utmost intensity. In this stage the actor has no need for self-control, no time for self-criticism. Abandon is everything.

Third stage: the actor has now acquired the necessary degree of emotional intensity. In order to perfect his accomplishment, he must check himself carefully, internally as well as externally. He must make sure that his actions not only are truthful and genuine but also that they will produce the effect for which he has been striving. When all this has been done most carefully, and all the corrections have been made, then the actor is ready for the final rehearsals.

2. ANALYTICAL THOUGHTS ON IAGO'S *CREDO* IN *OTELLO*

Iago has served under Otello for about fifteen years. He has served faithfully and efficiently, but is nevertheless passed over for promotion in favor of Cassio, who is closer to Otello's heart. Infuriated by his idol's betrayal of him, Iago builds up an insane craving for vengeance. It becomes increasingly clear to him that Otello must be destroyed at all costs.

At the beginning of the first act, Otello has just returned from the victorious battle against the Turks. Cassio, as the commander of the harbor garrison, has stayed at home. So has Iago, presumably for some unexplained military reason, but it can be assumed that he maneuvered his way into it to be able to lay the groundwork for his revenge.

After the return of Otello, Iago takes an active part in the celebration of the victory. He entices Cassio into getting drunk, knowing that Cassio will probably do something to disgrace himself. This actually happens and Cassio is demoted. But Iago is not yet satisfied. He is obsessed with the idea of destroying Otello. He ponders various ways of carrying out his plan. Then suddenly it occurs to him that Otello's greatest vulnerability lies in his love for Desdemona; the best, perhaps the only, way to destroy Otello is to make him jealous. This is why he sends Cassio into the garden to talk to Desdemona: if Otello sees Desdemona in the garden with Cassio, it will awaken his suspicion that Cassio is having an affair with her. If this suspicion can be strengthened by additional evidence, then the battle is won.

The first word of the *Credo* is "Vanne" (Go there!). Iago knows that Otello's destruction has been set in motion and that nothing can stop it. When he recognizes the monstrosity of this, he is terrified. He is *not* a villain; he is a man caught up in a pathological desire for vengeance. Here the "demon" enters. Iago, who still idolizes Otello in spite of the wrong, does not want to feel responsible for Otello's destruction. If he is being driven by a demon, then the demon can be blamed. Therefore he deifies the demon; he creates a god who cannot be denied. This is the only god to whom Iago can now address himself—the god that drives all men to evil simply because they are human.

3. THE BACKGROUND OF VIOLETTA'S ARIA
(What does "E strano" mean?)

Violetta is a courtesan. The most influential citizens of Paris frequent her house. She is in her twenties. Presumably, she was disappointed in love in her teens and in her disillusion became a prostitute, soon discovering that her sexual prowess gave her a tremendous power over men. She acquired more and more affluent clients until she became the leading courtesan of Paris, showered with men's attentions and leading a most pleasurable and luxurious life.

Her most important sponsor is Baron Douphol, about forty years old, a mystery man without a definite position but known everywhere, a participant in every political scheme. Douphol is not passionately in love with Violetta, but he utilizes her for political purposes and is therefore extremely jealous of her.

Gradually, Violetta becomes aware that she has consumption. She goes to Arosa in Switzerland for a cure, staying there for a year. When she hears that one of her rivals, Flora Bervoix, is slowly taking her place in Paris society, she is moved to action. With the immense energy that is characteristic of her she persuades the doctors that she is well and they dismiss her as cured.

The opening act of the opera shows her return to Paris society after a year's absence. This is a most important event for her: she must overwhelm her former friends immediately or her career is finished. As soon as the guests (some of whom had been detained at Flora's place, gambling) enter the salon, it is abundantly clear that Violetta is not only as beautiful as before but even more so. It is going to be a wonderful evening.

Gastone, who is a combination of court jester and master of ceremonies, has brought along, as a joke, a friend of his, Alfredo Germont, a young student from the provinces. Alfredo is a pleasant young man, but a bit awkward, totally unused to the ways of Paris society, and Gastone is amazed when everybody reacts to him favorably, even enthusiastically. Violetta herself is fascinated by this "joke," and she calls on Alfredo to sing a drinking song. Though terrified by her, he is spellbound, and sings a song that is sophisticated and suggestive. The guests respond with great fervor, and at the end of the song the atmosphere is charged with sexual excitement. Only the sudden playing of a brass band outside breaks the tension.

Violetta invites the guests to dance in the adjoining room. As she does so, she collapses. (Her collapse is brought on by a heart attack and not by her consumption, although this indirectly causes it; "cor pulmonare" is the medical term.) She is twice overcome. The guests want to know what ails her, but it is not sympathy that prompts them to ask; it is annoyance at being interrupted in their pleasures. Violetta, who wishes to be left alone because she is feeling worse than ever, is quite relieved when the guests move out of the room. She is not aware that Alfredo is hiding behind a curtain, waiting for the opportunity to talk to her alone. While Violetta looks into the mirror, shocked at her sickly appearance she notices Alfredo standing behind her. Ironically, she appears divinely beautiful to Alfredo when she knows that she looks her worst.

In the ensuing conversation Violetta struggles against feelings of passion for him. She tries to make light of his declarations of love but is unsuccessful. Her dilemma is grave: she sends Alfredo away, but knows in her heart that she does not want him to leave. Instinctively, she hands him a camellia, not suspecting what it will lead to. Actually, the camellia turns out to be the instrument that brings him back to her.

During the duet with Alfredo, Violetta's state of mind changes completely. She is now seriously interested in another human being, something that has never happened before. When the guests come in to take their leave, she is already so far removed from her former world that she is revolted by every word and every gesture of these people.

Therefore: "E strano" (It is strange). "How is it possible that I now despise these people—the same people who were so dear to me only a short while ago?"

24

Felsenstein's Magic Realism

by H. H. Stuckenschmidt

(A review of the premiere of *The Tales of Hoffmann* at the Komische Oper, which appeared in the *Frankfurter Allgemeine Zeitung* on January 30, 1958. Hans Heinz Stuckenschmidt is one of the best-known contemporary German writers on music, particularly noted for his writing on Schönberg and twelve-tone composition.)

This work has clearly been missing in Felsenstein's repertory. The boldest of our creative stage directors did a great deal of planning in order to present it. He went back to the sources: to the play *Les Contes d'Hoffmann* by Jules Barbier and Michel Carré, and from there to the tales of E. T. A. Hoffmann himself: *Der Sandmann, Don Juan, Phantasiestücke in Callot's Manier,* and *Serapionsbrüder.* He wrote a new, iambic text to replace the usual translation, and he removed the recitatives and a few superfluous musical numbers. His musical collaborator, Karl-Fritz Voigtmann, interpolated a song from the operetta *Maître Peronilla* in the Olympia act, and he adorned some of the spoken dialogue with background music by Offenbach.*

All this, as well as the inclusion of the connecting action with

*A brief reminder, with proper apologies to the erudite, that E. T. A. Hoffmann (1776–1822) was a German poet and composer whose name was a household word during his lifetime. While his music has more or less been forgotten, his fantastic short stories are still widely read by the German-speaking public.

Hoffmann's Muse, who transforms herself into his servant Niklaus, was done according to Offenbach and his sources. But now the real function of the stage director begins. And through his work, *The Tales of Hoffmann* has become almost a different opera. This evening at the Komische Oper belongs among the most remarkable, the ones most filled with inner contradictions, that I have experienced in Felsenstein's theater, and that is quite a statement!

You see cones of light crossing each other in space. Suddenly a human figure is lighted; the face of a singer appears in quasi close-up. Brightest light changes abruptly to deep darkness, in which a few moving lamps lead you to surmise that the terrified guests have begun a search for Olympia's thief. The same darkness occurs after the courtesan dies of poisoning, and it is eerily pierced by the whimpers of the toadlike dwarf Pitichinaccio. When the Muse changes her clothes, male garments fly to her out of the sky, and the tulle which she sheds disappears in the same ghostly fashion. The stage machinery works with a breathtaking tightness and accuracy, one visual effect outdoes the other, and Rudolf Heinrich's baroque fantasy of colors and shapes conjures up an imaginary world in which naturalism and magic illusion are resplendently wedded to each other.*

On this colorful and magic realism Felsenstein superimposes a fantastic world of caricatured types. The characters, in their shadowy peculiarity, leave the realm of E. T. A. Hoffmann far behind. It is a surrealist painter's dream, replete with sinister figures burlesquing themselves, part of a twilight world of shocking allure. There is not one type, one entrance, or one gesture that is not shaped by Felsenstein himself; the performer is the raw material on which the demoniacal director imposes his artistic will. Characters such as the servant Franz in the house of the moribund Antonia—a deaf and senile instrument of fate who in his solitude inexplicably starts to sing, and then falls to the ground: a weirdness that one will not easily forget. Werner End-

*See page 161.

ers acts this scene overwhelmingly. Or the entrance of Coppelius, the maker of eyeglasses, with his Berlin-Jewish inflection and his Biedermier makeup—a character portrayal of the first order, to which Rudolf Asmus cannot add anything further in his portrayals of Doctor Miracle and Dappertutto.

Melitta Muszely sings the three women, as well as their synthesis, Stella. Felsenstein has radically reduced the doll to a dead mechanism; even her aria sounds broken, chopped up in an exaggerated staccato like a barrel organ. Set into a twofold opposition, against the glass and metal machinery, and against the courtly assemblage of guests—the babbling ladies with their bustles—this tender robot appears totally imbued with the spirit of E. T. A. Hoffmann, a product of science at whose death the limbs pathetically drop to the floor.

But Antonia becomes a caricature. Hysterically she unleashes her anger on the keyboard of her harpsichord; furiously she tries to force singing out of her decaying body. The "tourterelle" (turtledove) has turned into a Callas impeded by tuberculosis. Although flawlessly sung, it is the exact opposite of what we love in the character of Antonia.

Then there is Venice. On quivering waters the gondola approaches a Moorish portal; the chorus, which has been placed in the orchestra pit, sings a barcarole; a woman steps out of the boat and glides into the palace. The curtain opens on a luxurious hall. A canopy with heavy red velvet draperies, Greek sculptures, a dwarf dressed in the colorful squares of a jester's costume. Giulietta has become a tintype from the Comédie française. With bombastic elocution and exaggerated showmanship she portrays love. All this has been clothed in a mantle of screaming melodramatics, blinding, like the colors of this luxury bordello. The performers have been deprived of any trace of naturalness; stylization triumphs in a grossly overdone formalism that strives almost beyond its own boundaries. The spectator is overpowered by visual effects that chase one another; a separate set has been interpolated for the short scene of the duel, which is followed by the last and lethal confrontation in the boudoir of Giulietta.

Epilogue: Quoting Felsenstein

As must have become clear from some of the foregoing, Felsenstein is not a stage director in the ordinary sense. While most directors spend practically all their time on the physical arrangement of stage movements—"blocking" is the term commonly used—this arrangement, although painstakingly prepared on his part, happens with Felsenstein almost as an afterthought. His most determined effort goes into preparing the spiritual concept with each individual member of the cast—not in the sense of instructing him in what to do, but rather helping him to find his own approach toward a goal that has been discussed and agreed upon by all participants. The method is of necessity new and different with every new performer. For that reason, the Komische Oper keeps very accurate and detailed rehearsal reports, in which these statements and conversations are recorded.

Felsenstein's remarks during early rehearsals, always made on the spur of the moment and sometimes purposely exaggerated in order to produce a stronger reaction, present perhaps the best clue to what makes him different from other directors, and what makes his performers so clear and direct in their effect on the audience.

* *

Do not turn your attention to yourself—always to your partner.

* *

You must not do anything in a vague manner; everything in the theater can and *must* be expressed in specific terms.

* *

The actor finds a character not by striving to be that character but by identifying with the character's actions and desires.

* *

In speaking the same is true as in singing: speaking fast does not necessarily indicate *inner* tempo, rather the opposite.

* *

[To a singer rehearsing Pamina, at the end of the Pamina-Papageno duet]: Imagine that the coloraturas at the end of the duet are not composed—they are merely a lack of discipline on your part. But you are so happy that you *must* sing them.

* *

In the theater you are always told that you must be intense. That is nonsense. It results in an artificial tempo rather than one based on your inner condition. "Intensity" is the death of all expression, because it is a substitute for content.

* *

During rehearsals, you must always be *above* the image that you are trying to create. You must produce an inner exaltation, even if in view of the complexity of the task you do not quite feel it.

* *

There is no singing without Eros.

* *

[During the rehearsals for *Tales of Hoffmann*]: In such a fantastic piece the fantastic element must not be furnished by the decor.

It can only be hinted at, so that the characters of the work remain in the foreground. Their actions more than anything else produce the fantastic quality which stirs the imagination of the spectator.

* *

At first [in rehearsal] you should be satisfied with what you have accomplished. If you demand too much from yourself, the result will be tenseness, and then you may even lose what you have already accomplished.

* *

Since the singer sings with compressed breath, there is a tendency to let the phrases fly off into exalted recitation. What is needed is the courage to take a breath, to tear the sentence apart. Then a verbal action will be created. The result should be a seamless unity, with the action in the center; there must be a unity of condition and expression.

* *

What is most important is not the words, but what is between the words, and what can be accomplished by the words.

* *

In our work, we must not think initially about the audience or about the "effect." This is a basic rule of the realistic music theater. Rather, we must start with the character, and with the situation as it is shown in the drama.

* *

Do not gamble on success, but work toward it.

Biographical Note

Walter Felsenstein was born in Vienna in 1901, and trained to be an actor. His first theater engagements in Germany (Lübeck, Mannheim, Beuthen), beginning in 1923, were as an actor; but soon he took over directing assignments, first of plays, then also of operas, beginning with *La Bohème* and *Fidelio.* His first major engagement as a stage director was in Basel, Switzerland, where between 1927 and 1929 he staged nineteen plays and sixteen operas (among the latter *Meistersinger, Orfeo, Traviata, Ariadne,* and *Turandot.*) After several years as director in Freiburg, he was engaged as first stage director of opera in Cologne in 1932. In the two years that he spent there his work began to attract international attention.

During the following years he staged a number of productions in Frankfurt and Berlin, but in rather insecure circumstances, since he had been excluded from the Reichstheaterkammer (the official organization of all stage employees in the Third Reich). In 1938 he accepted an offer from Zurich, where he stayed until 1940, staging many operas and operettas. After that, the famous actor Heinrich George brought him to the Schiller Theater in Berlin, which had been shielded against Nazi influence. In 1941 and '42 he staged a number of productions in Aachen, with Herbert von Karajan as conductor. Also, his staging of *Figaro* at the 1942 Salzburg Festival attracted wide attention.

Shortly after the end of the war a group of performers gathered in Berlin to create a stage for "light musical dramas," and Felsenstein was put in charge of the project. The result of this was what we now know as the Komische

Oper, and after twenty-seven years and innumerable successes Felsenstein is still head of the organization. He has also staged many productions abroad, notably at La Scala in Milan, in Hamburg and Moscow, and at the Schwetzingen Summer Festival.

WHITMAN COLLEGE LIBRARY